The Numerology of Relationships

Decode Your Love Life Through the Power of Numbers

CARMEN HARRA

JAICO PUBLISHING HOUSE
Ahmedabad Bangalore Chennai
Delhi Hyderabad Kolkata Mumbai

Published by Jaico Publishing House
A-2 Jash Chambers, 7-A Sir Phirozshah Mehta Road
Fort, Mumbai - 400 001
jaicopub@jaicobooks.com
www.jaicobooks.com

Published in arrangement with
REDFeather Mind, Body, Spirit
An imprint of Schiffer Publishing, Ltd.
4880 Lower Valley Road
Atglen, PA 19310

To be sold only in India

THE NUMEROLOGY OF RELATIONSHIPS
ISBN 978-93-49358-72-0

Original English language edition published as
Plus One: The Numerology of Relationships

First Jaico Impression: 2025

Printed by
Nutech Print Services - India, New Delhi

I dedicate this book
to Virgil,
my favorite

NUMBER ONE

CONTENTS

INTRODUCTION

There is geometry in the
humming of the strings.
There is music in the spacing
of the spheres.
—Pythagoras

NUMBERS ARE THE LANGUAGE OF THE UNIVERSE; they are the medium through which Spirit speaks to us, encourages us, warns us, and reminds of our higher nature. In the physical world, we use numbers every day, from phones to bank accounts, but what many people don't realize is that each of us was born with a unique set of numbers that foretells our fate. This numerological code was established on the day you took your first breath and contains your divine DNA. Just as you have a genetic makeup, so too do we possess a spiritual composition that can reveal the full scope of your destiny.

Every number is a microcosm of its own, carrying specific attributes and qualities. Numerology lends meaning to our dominant numbers and applies them to our day-to-day lives. Numbers are a form of energy, and because we are energetic beings, they convert our thoughts, emotions, and actions. This magic relationship lies at the very heart of psychology, imbued with metaphysics. Its founding fathers, Sigmund Freud and Carl Jung, among others, recognized the immutable connection between earth and cosmos as expressed through numbers.

As an intuitive psychologist, relationship expert, and numerologist for 30 years, I can tell you that our lives are greatly swayed by our divine codes and that our relationships are especially commanded by numbers. *The Numerology of Relationships* examines the ways in which numbers manifest throughout a love relationship. It's no coincidence that you met a special someone on a particular date, that you have an inexplicable but incessant attraction to him or her, or that the numbers in your birthdays blend perfectly. Furthermore, numerology can also shed light on why you felt an initial attraction to someone that faded quickly or why your relationship with a person turned utterly toxic. It can clarify the reason your marriage ended suddenly or lasted a fixed amount of time. This science of numbers can explain the fluctuating energy of relationships that reaches far beyond free will or common sense.

As it turns out, numbers account for much more than the level of compatibility at play between two people. Most numerology books outline compatibility from one angle: the present. *The Numerology of Relationships* delves into past lives shared by you and your partner and whether your numbers indicate karma carried over into the present that may affect your relationship well into the future, in good or bad ways. I offer an innovative method to determine whether past-life karma is at play between you and your significant other, and how you can resolve it to give your relationship the best opportunity to succeed.

I organized this book to include not only the meaning of your life path number but the archetype it represents. We each adhere to an archetype that is embedded into our subconscious mind. They are part of our higher design and are responsible for our strengths, weaknesses, inclinations, and behaviors. Your archetype steers you toward certain types of partners and dictates the decisions you make in relationships. If your life path number is 1, for example, your archetype is the Independent, since this number is associated with autonomy and ambition. This means your personality is characterized by a strong sense of identity, a need to do things on your own, and a reluctance to give part of yourself to another person. You can imagine that some of these traits aren't the most favorable to maintain an enduring bond with another person. But *The Numerology of Relationships* teaches you how to mitigate tendencies that might be harmful to your relationship so that you can break out of the limitations of your numerological archetype and achieve the commitment you want and deserve. Understanding the archetype associated with your life path number, as well as your partner's, defines your dynamic and potential.

Numbers are predictive of how a relationship is likely to unfold in time; initial compatibility can be traced through numerology, but so can long-term love. My book analyzes every combination of life path numbers on the basis of the seven kinds of relationships that exist. These seven relationship types include transitory, toxic, stagnant, compromise, complementary, karmic, and soulmate. Some numbers, such as 1 and 1, are complementary matches that can make it work with a bit of effort. Some, such as 5 and 6, brew toxicity and cause much suffering for both partners. Others, such as 1 and 9, denote a soulmate bond that's unlikely to be disturbed by external influences. *The Numerology of Relationships* weaves through each numerological match in great detail, granting you awareness about the type of relationship you can expect to have with your love interest, and its challenges and obstacles, in addition to its advantages and resources.

The Numerology of Relationships discloses the hidden knowledge behind numbers and how they materialize in our love lives. It's a numerology manual that decodes human relationships on a groundbreaking level. Through its comprehensive style and easy-to-follow format, readers can interpret their numerological archetype,

CHAPTER ONE

THE LANGUAGE OF THE UNIVERSE

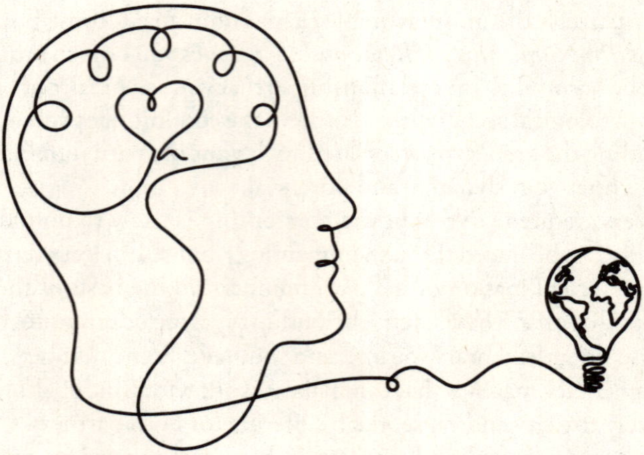

The stars in the heavens sing a music if only we had ears to hear.

—Pythagoras

MANY PEOPLE HAVE A NUMBER IN MIND that they think brings luck to them. Some people look at the clock and see 11:11 every night and believe it's validation of their guardian angel watching over them. Some like the number 8 because it symbolizes infinity or the number 7 because it carries religious connotations. Others celebrate a specific day of the year, perhaps one on which their child was born or a family member passed. We all take the liberty to attach meaning to numbers, often without knowing the actual meaning of numbers. Many of us don't know that 2 has a very different energy than 3, for example, or that a life path 5 and a life path 6 theoretically shouldn't be in a love relationship. Most of us choose to learn about only those numbers that hold special meaning for us, but only by studying the full spectrum of numbers can we expose their secrets.

Everything in the universe vibrates at a fixed frequency and is expressed in the physical world through energy. Each number has its own personality and individual ideals it represents. Numbers are expressions of energy and the means through which the universe communicates with us. St. Augustine of Hippo wrote that "numbers are the universal language offered by the deity to humans as confirmation of the truth." He believed that everything in the universe had a relationship with numbers and that it was our duty to translate the truths of numbers as they manifested into reality. As a species, we have been acknowledging this fact for tens of thousands of years: ancient cultures deemed numerology as one of the paths to unity with God and the celestial sphere. As far back as 30,000 years ago, Egyptians etched marks into bones to track the phases of the moon. Ancient Babylonians represented movements of the planets through numbers, which they then used to predict astronomical phenomena such as eclipses. Cultures around the world still venerate numbers as more than numerical assignments and attach special significance to each digit.

In its simplest definition, numerology is the study of numbers and their effects on people and the world around them. The history of numerology is vast and complex, but it's usually divided into three branches: Eastern, Indian, and Western. There exist other schools of numerology, but these are the main three. Eastern, or Chaldean, numerology originated in ancient Babylon and is the oldest system. Indian, or Vedic, numerology links numbers with cosmic powers and planets. Western numerology is the most ubiquitous. It's also called the Pythagorean system and dates to around 500 BCE in Greece. This method examines the traits of single digits 1 through 9 and is the one we'll study in this book.

Without numerology, we wouldn't have the number systems we know and use today. Ancient Greek culture integrated numerology into its mathematical studies and devised geometry, algebra, and axiomatic arithmetic—areas of math that largely shape and organize our modern world. Pythagoras was credited with the creation of Western numerology after he speculated that there was a relationship between numbers and musical notes. He was fascinated with numbers and thought that all things could be rendered into numerical form; it has even been documented that he traveled to Egypt to study Chaldean numerology for 22 years.

Believing that numbers can identify the nature both of humans and the natural world, Pythagoras devised a way to produce accurate descriptions of individual personalities. He and other prominent figures of the time believed that mathematical concepts were more practical than physical ones and had greater actuality in the world. This theory was adopted by other philosophers, mathematicians, and theologians and became known as Pythagoreanism, a religious sect that theorized that the universe was based on numerical harmony. Pythagoreanism was a mixture of prescience and mysticism and the basis for many of the virtues we uphold today, including moral responsibility, universal tolerance, and modest living. Pythagoras's principles spread in popularity and eventually diffused into a global belief.

YOUR FIRST GIFT

Many factors were decided when you were born: your gender, height, weight, and eye color—even the amount of hair on your head. What was likely not taken into consideration (unless your parents were numerologists) was the role that numbers would play in your life. When my daughter Alexandra was born on November 9, 1986, I quickly calculated her birth code amid my joyful exhaustion. She had a 2 (11) in her month, representing the mother figure, so I knew she would remain close to me throughout her life. The 9 in her day of birth signified that she would want to do good for others, and the 6 in her year of birth (the sum of 1986) gifted her with balance and stability. Together, these numbers equaled her life path, an 8. Yes, she would be grounded, successful, and pragmatic. This was what my mind resolved as I stared into her glittering brown eyes for the first time. Any other mother would have been frozen with awe at the tiny miracle she was holding in that moment, but me, I pondered on what my daughter's numbers determined for her future. They were, after all, her gift.

Numerology isn't some far-fetched, abstract theory; it's a universal law that applies to all of us. Your birthday, too, gave you copious gifts when you entered this world. Your date of birth awarded you many of the things that you are today: your career, talents, tendencies, ambitions, health, love life, family, karmic patterns, and obstacles you were meant to overcome—these elements were predetermined for you before you were born. In many ways, your birthday handed you your destiny. From there, it became up to you to make something great of it.

I have recognized this fact since I was a little girl, being captivated by surreal matters before I even understood them well. Before I learned about spirituality, I was subconsciously aware of a reality beyond the one I could experience with my five senses. It was like an endless world waiting to be discovered, and I, for one, couldn't wait to unravel its mysteries. I was in third grade when I had a premonition about my grandfather passing . . . 30 minutes before my father walked into my classroom and pulled me into the hallway to give me the sad news. I remember perusing old, tattered volumes on Allan Kardec, the father of spiritism, in the library of my high school in a small town in Romania while my classmates were studying math and science. In my first year of college, I started compiling numerology charts for my girlfriends on the basis of their birthdays. As a life path 9, I knew I would immerse myself in metaphysics for as long as my soul occupied this body.

My thirst for higher knowledge took me to unimaginable places. Over the span of 30 years, I've been able to help tens of thousands of clients from all over the globe uncover their calling and invite more joy, passion, and purpose into their lives. By using my own gifts to my advantage, I crafted a career out of my intuition and obsession with numbers, coupled with vast teachings developed in ancient times. Seventeen years ago, I wrote *Decoding Your Destiny*, a book on numerology that quickly became a bestseller. That was my second book in a series of (so far) nine books on self-help and spirituality.

As I weave through life day after day, I continue to sense the transcendent and unbreakable thread that connects all things, right down to you, who are a gift in your own right. I believe that life starts to take on new meaning once you become aware of your unique set of numbers and what they unveil about your past, present, and future. Collectively, we are reawakening to metaphysical arts such as numerology that infuse our lives with sacred synchronicity and go far beyond the laws of logic.

A DIVINE DNA

In biology class, you probably learned that you have a set of genes that were passed down to you from your parents. Within your DNA are instructions for creating a complete you: your blood type, the color of your skin, the size of your feet, the number of your eyelashes, and all minute details that make up your physical being are included in your genes. What you may not know is that you also have a spiritual DNA encoded within your being. This divine code describes you entirely and is a complete record of you. It explains your tendencies, strengths, weaknesses, talents, and much more. It offers the sum of who you are, both the experiences you inherited from your ancestors and the new possibilities you can project within your lifetime. I believe it is as important to know your numerology as it is to know your biology; understanding your numbers is an integral part of self-awareness.

Numerology can help you glide through all of life's twists and turns with grace. It can reveal your soul's evolution and the karmic patterns you carried into this lifetime, as well as your ties to some members of your family and not others (this is why some people have parents they've never even met and have no connection to!). In terms of love relationships, you can find out almost everything you need to know about your partner, effectively "reading his record," if you have his name and birthday handy. You can even acknowledge the existence of past-life karma with your significant other. Before you move from your home or job, you can conclude whether it's the right time for a big change or whether you should wait until the optimal year rolls back around. You can also prevent and treat conditions you may be predisposed to, on the basis of your numerology. Your birthday can even forecast your time of death (understandably, you may not want to know this piece of information). If you recognize the meaning of your numbers, you can know what to anticipate and what to avoid.

Your birthday spells out your contract with the universe, which you agreed to as a soul on the other side before reincarnating. You may amend your contract, but only to an extent: many of the events and situations inscribed within your birthday will find a way of manifesting. This is what your soul signed up for. It's no coincidence that your spirit picked a precise moment to enter this world. In the instant that you took your first breath, life surged through you and sealed your pact with the universe. This is referenced in the book of Genesis, which describes this phenomenon as God "breathed into his nostrils the breath of life, and the man became a living being." You were meant to be born at a certain time, in a certain part of the world, and into a certain family. For the most part, you will have to pass through the situations that were set up for you long before you reincarnated. These are your individual lessons to help you resolve your karma on Earth and liberate your soul.

You also have free will, of course, so if you don't like what your numerology says about you, you have every right to try to change it. Numerology empowers you to reach a thorough realization of your preappointed course and the capacity of your volition. Let's say that, according to your numbers, you're supposed to go through a divorce in this lifetime. You want to avoid this, so you choose your partner carefully and put extra effort into resolving the problems in your relationship instead of separating. In this way, you evade the divorce and alter the course of your life. To invert the scenario, you might soon realize that you're unhappy with your partner and there's no fixing the relationship; separation is the only remedy. This satisfies the prophecy set up by your numbers and puts you on the course chosen for you. You'll still meet the people you're fated to meet along the way. You'll still have the possibility of being in a relationship with the partner who will challenge you, but whether you choose to stay with him is up to you. You can use your free will to *reinforce* or *reverse* your destiny, to act in favor of or against it; the path you take depends on the decisions you take and the ways in which you interact with the universe. You can choose to fulfill your potential completely or only halfway, to ignite the fire of possibility within you or leave the embers glowing weakly. Either way, knowing your numbers provides critical insight into why you're here and where you're meant to go.

In reading this book, there's a chance that you'll learn about your life path and archetype and think, "That doesn't sound like me at all!" If that's the case, it may be that you've effectuated your spiritual responsibilities and evolved to vibrate at the highest frequency for your numbers. If you're a Free Spirit (life path 5) but you've been able to uphold a long-term relationship, it means you've overcome the commitment obstacles of this particular number. It can also be that you still have lessons to learn to embody the role of your life path. If you're an Extrovert (life path 3) but you have trouble expressing yourself to others, this is something you need to work on, since communication should come easily to you. People change with time, but their numbers don't. This means you're free to ascend to the highest potential for your archetype or, conversely, descend to its lowest depths. You're free to roam within the spectrum of your life path's characteristics. By introspecting and being perfectly honest with yourself, you can discover your current strengths and weaknesses and transform yourself to your liking.

THE PSYCHOLOGY BEHIND NUMBERS

Numerology books usually lay out a person's attributes. Readers appreciate receiving insight into themselves, but they might want to know what to do with this knowledge. I decided to take it a step further and teach you how to work with your many facets: how to heighten your innate strengths, minimize your weaknesses, curb harmful tendencies, and become the best version of you both inside and outside a relationship. Numerology and psychology share a symbiotic relationship. One stems from the other: a person's divine code requires psychological interpretation, and a person's way of thinking can be explained by their numbers. They are complementary studies because where one leaves off, the other picks up. I aim to take numerology to a higher level and use it as a psychological instrument to interpret your love personality and improve your chances of building the relationship you want and deserve.

Human beings can exhibit extensive personality traits. We are born possessing every trait identified thus far by psychology. Why, then, do we display some and not others? Why does each person have a personality that's unique to him or her? Our personality is shaped not only by the divine DNA with which we enter this world but also by the experiences through which we pass in life. But who or what arranges the experiences that mold our character, both directly and indirectly? Our numbers. Here, the impact of numerology comes full circle: our numbers are responsible both for the way we think and significant events in our life that frame the way we think.

The benefit of numerology is that it can explain how a person does the things he does, while the payoff of psychology is that it can explain why he does these things. Numerology explains how; psychology explains why. In conjunction, these two studies present a thorough interpretation of each type of individual and his behaviors: his actions and nonactions, his wishes and desires, and his fears and trepidations.

AN OVERVIEW OF YOUR MONTH, DAY, AND YEAR OF BIRTH

The day, month, and year you were born clarifies multiple aspects of your fate. Each of these three numbers represents a distinct part of your being. Let's look at them individually:

The day of your birth is your identity. It discloses the image you choose to portray to the world and the way people perceive you when they first meet you. Your birth day establishes your integrity and personal power as well as the unique authority you hold over others.

The month of your birth is your trajectory. It highlights your overall direction in life, specifically in regard to your career and calling. It can illuminate your greater purpose and what you're meant to do, your potential and possibilities at different junctures in life. Your birth month outlines the elements that bring you luck and usher you down the road the universe has paved for you.

The year of your birth is the universal influence over your life. It defines your life lessons and the karmic debts you returned to resolve in this lifetime. Your birth year serves as the accumulation of your soul's memory: the challenges you must face, the people you're supposed to meet, and the greater themes that will inevitably play out.

These three components of your birthday are added together to reveal your soul code, which exemplifies the totality of who you are.

YOUR SOUL CODE

The sum of your day, month, and year of birth constitutes your life path, or soul code. It indicates your temperament and physical vulnerabilities. It can also unearth hidden talents and natural abilities you didn't know you had. Your soul code is composed not only of the numbers you have, but by the numbers you're missing. We're all missing some numbers from our code; no birthday contains every number from 1 through 9, because each one of us is passing through a process of evolution. The very fact that your soul has chosen to reincarnate is proof that you're still undergoing the cycle of completion. Missing numbers are sometimes more telling than existing numbers because they accentuate the lessons you will have to learn throughout life. For example, if you're missing a 5 from your birthday, you might not have had a father figure growing up, or you had to go through a separation from your spouse. It is extremely soul satisfying to cultivate qualities you're lacking, to fill in the gaps left by missing numbers. You will find it immensely rewarding to work on independence if you're missing a 1, introspection if you're missing a 2, communication if you're missing a 3, and so on. By examining both the numbers you have and the numbers you don't, you can piece together a complete puzzle of your soul's standing and the journey that awaits you on Earth.

Jewish Kabbalah is a set of esoteric teachings meant to explain the relationship between the eternal God and the finite universe. The ancient Kabbalists acknowledged that numbers govern our emotions, karma, health, and, notably, our relationships. They recognized that every number is made up of a specific energy, and associated each digit from 1 through 9 with a planet. Ancient Greeks, the inventors of Western numerology, also attributed numbers 1 through 9 to planets as they were understood at that time. This includes the sun and moon, which the Greeks took to mean celestial objects. In astrology, every planet exerts a particular influence over us. On the basis of the movements of each planet through our solar system, during some months one planet may have a more dominant energy than others. If the planet that corresponds to the main number in your soul code is weak during a certain month, the universe will not be supportive of your efforts on that month. For example, if your life path is a 1, your energy is that of the sun, and this means that warmer months, such as March, April, July, and August, are far more conducive months than months such as October, November, or December, when the sun's impact on the earth is weaker.

To calculate your soul code, start with your date of birth. Add the numbers of the month you were born (January is 1, February is 2, March is 3, and so on). Reduce months with two digits to a single digit, like so: October is 1 (1 + 0 = 1), November is 2 (1 + 1 = 2), and December is 3 (1 + 2 = 3).

Next, tally the numbers of the day you were born. If you were born on a day with double digits, add them together. If you were born on the 29th, add 2 + 9 = 11, then 1 + 1 = 2. Or if you were born on the 30th, add 3 + 0 = 3.

Then add the four digits of your birth year. If you were born in 1974, add 1 + 9 + 7 + 4 = 21, then 2 + 1 = 3.

Finally, add the three numbers from your month, day, and year of birth together. If you get a two-digit number, add the individual digits to reduce it to a single digit. This is called a pure or primary number.

Let's say Mary was born on May 21, 1988. Her month equals a 5, her day equals a 3 (2 + 1 = 3), and her year equals an 8 (1 + 9 + 8 + 8 = 8). Her life path is a 7 (5 + 3 + 8 = 16, then 1 + 6 = 7).

Apply the above steps to calculate your life path number, then study the brief outline of each life path number according to traditional numerology. In the following chapters, I'll provide thorough explanations of the life paths as they correspond to archetypes.

Life path 1: independent, ambitious, and a born leader
Influence of number 1: attitude
Famous number 1s: Martin Luther King Jr., Larry King, Tom Hanks

Life path 1s are administrated by the sun, which rules our solar system. They hold the energy of leadership and acumen. Because of this energy, 1s not only have lots of ideas, they also have the self-discipline to carry them out. Ambitious and fearless, 1s are natural leaders. They like to learn and are often self-taught, then they like to pass on their knowledge to others. 1s are hardworking, smart, organized, neat, and extremely productive. They genuinely enjoy waking up at sunrise and starting the day on the right foot. People with this life path are driven by their own convictions and are pioneers in many different fields. Beliefs like these endow them with radiant positivity and a can-do attitude.

In terms of their relationships, 1s have great social abilities. They might have to deal with a domineering parent during childhood, which makes them want to become independent and live on their own from early on in life. They're generally healthy and energetic, regularly working on their fitness. Their health can suffer when they work too much, which they tend to do.

Favorable periods for 1s are months when the sun is strong (March, April, July, and August). Less favorable months are months when the sun is weak, such as October, November, and December.

According to Kabbalah, the sun is associated with the head and rules the right eye, the right side of the body, and the left hemisphere of the brain. Physically, 1s are most vulnerable in these areas and are likely to have headaches, bone fractures, and arthritis.

Those with this life path may have difficulty conveying love and their emotions, which can affect their relationships. They can be hardheaded, overly cautious about money, jealous, and overcritical.

People who are missing 1 from their soul code must foster independence, courage, identity, self-awareness, hard work, creative thinking, motivation, and problem-solving.

Life path 2: emotional, reserved, and intuitive
Influence of number 2: introspection
Famous number 2s: Madonna, Barack Obama, Bill Clinton

Number 2s are represented by the moon, which reflects light from the sun and emits the maternal energy of cooperation, balance, partnership, and understanding. 2s tend to be good listeners and are diplomatic and tactful. They are often quiet, introverted, humble, intelligent, and calm. Those with a life path 2 should work on realizing their dreams, heightening their intellect, keeping close relationships, and enjoying leisure time. They tend to be romantic, but only when they open up and trust their partner. Otherwise, they're not particularly demonstrative. Number 2s usually have family members who judge them, and as a result they grow up with low self-esteem.

Strong periods for 2s are June and July. Weak periods are December, January, and February. The moon rules over the left eye, the left side of the body, and the right hemisphere of the brain, in addition to the neck, which exposes 2s to sore throats, tonsillitis, and thyroid problems. The moon is associated with emotions, so 2s can suffer from nervous conditions and indigestion.

This number can be superstitious and restless, becoming rebellious when restricted. People with this life path can be emotional and insecure, repressing their feelings and doubting themselves. When they do express themselves, their words can come out the wrong way. The challenge for 2s is to feel emotionally safe enough to be in a relationship.

Those who don't have a number 2 in their soul code must learn how to create and maintain good relationships and build trust, security, and intimacy. They should work on setting boundaries, learning to communicate, and giving support to others. Women who are missing 2 also must learn the lesson of motherhood: they may have difficulty becoming a mother or relating to their mother or daughter. Men who are missing 2 lack female energy, meaning they might have trouble finding a wife, lose or have a distant relationship with their mother, or pass through the loss of a female figure in their life.

Life path 3: creative, outgoing, and charismatic
Influence of number 3: communication
Famous number 3s: Jennifer Lopez, Hillary Clinton, Barbara Walters

Number 3 carries the energy of Jupiter, the planet of courage, persuasion, hard work, energy, and knowledge. It is considered a lucky planet and bears a powerful energy. Life path 3 is the number of creativity, beauty, and "the good life." 3s are extroverted and gifted with eloquence and musical talents. They often have lovely voices and take up careers in the arts, media, or education. They are well informed, altruistic, and extravagant. Those with a 3 code are naturally honest, trustworthy, appreciative, and observant. They love to receive attention and try their hand at interior design.

Favorable periods for 3s are February, March, and December. Less favorable periods are October and November.

Jupiter rules the area between the waist and the thighs, so 3s are given to liver, kidney, and skin problems as well as emotional disturbances. People with this life path number display moodiness, impulsivity, hasty decision-making, vengefulness, and secrecy. They can become easily angered.

For someone who is missing this number from his code, it's advisable to learn self-expression and creativity and to master the artistic self. This lesson encompasses being in touch with your inner world and your dreams, appreciating imagination, and balancing life's demands with ingenuity and agility.

Life path 4: orderly, pragmatic, and self-reliant
Influence of number 4: logic
Famous number 4s: Donald Trump, Bill Gates, Oprah Winfrey

Number 4 bears the energy of Uranus, the planet of discipline, grounding, and structure; 4s are active, dynamic, diplomatic, self-motivated, determined, caring, brave, and generous. They tend to have a good memory and a superior sense of dignity, which can make 4s seem a bit egoistic to outsiders. Those with a life path 4 know the merit of working hard to achieve wealth and power, and they often do so through inheritance or real estate. They're interested in inventing new ways of doing things and being remembered for them. Members of this life path are calculated and realistic, sometimes to an exaggerated degree.

Strong periods for 4s are March, April, July, and August. Weak periods are October, November, and December.

Uranus rules the heart, and 4s may be struck by ailments in the head or chest, bone disorders, and backaches. 4s need to work on keeping their emotions under control and mitigating their ego, frustration, aggression, and haughtiness. They should also learn to give others the benefit of the doubt more often and recognize that they don't always know best.

People who are missing 4 from their soul code must learn the lessons of achievement through planning, hard work, and discipline. They should also try to apply reasoning and rationale more often.

Life path 5: free spirited, adventurous, and versatile
Influence of number 5: freedom
Famous number 5s: Abraham Lincoln, Angelina Jolie, Steven Spielberg

Number 5 is commanded by the planet Mercury, which holds dominion over intellect, independence, and freedom. Number 5s are strong-willed risk takers who appreciate their freedom above all. They're intelligent beings with deep feelings, good physical energy, and strong intuition; 5s are shrewd, progressive, and adaptable. Those within this life path are elevated thinkers who like to think outside the box and even step outside the box; they have a penchant to travel, dabble in the arts, and attain luxurious objects. Number 5s also love to dream and try new activities. This erects blocks in becoming attached to people for long periods of time. In love, they crave personal space. They tend to marry later in life and have few or no children because they have trouble being tied down. Their greatest problems arise from their stubborn aptitude and inability to be intimate with another person.

Favorable periods for 5s are May, June, August, and most of September. Weak periods are the end of September and December.

Mercury is the planet associated with the lungs, so 5s may have problems with their airways or difficulty with breathing. They tend to have recurring infections in the ear and neck or liver problems, together with constipation. Despite this, 5s usually live long lives.

People who are missing 5 from their soul code must learn to adapt to sudden changes, be more generous, take care of their health, and attain freedom. Because 5 is a male energy, women who are missing 5 often have blocks in finding a husband or are missing the male figure in some way, such as not having their father present in their youth. A woman may be able to find this male energy by having a son and a man who lacks this number has to learn the lesson of becoming a father and being a son.

Life path 6: empathetic, loving, and humble
Influence of number 6: sacrifice
Famous number 6s: Albert Einstein, Eleanor Roosevelt, George W. Bush

The energy of Venus leads number 6, the planet of service, responsibility, emotional harmony, and nurturing. Number 6s are kind, polite, soft spoken, funny, temperamental, friendly, humorous, sacrificial, and talkative. They have lots of ideas, an active mind, and a passion for life; 6s are concerned for others and possess a strong need to assist and serve. They simply adore the family life and feel an unfailing sense of duty toward members of their kin.

Strong periods for 6s are April, September, and most of October. Weak periods are the end of October, November, and January.

Venus rules the stomach and genital area, so 6s are most vulnerable to stomach and urinary problems, gallstones, and venereal diseases, and, moreover, congestion.

This number needs to work on their negative thoughts, anxiety, dark moods, and angry outbursts. They are easily bored, fussy, narrow minded, and fragile and take a long time to heal. They can appease these tendencies by working on meaningful projects.

People who are missing 6 from their soul code need to learn lessons of family, home, being loved for who they are, and service to society.

Life path 7: inquisitive, spiritual, and deep
Influence of number 7: knowledge
Famous number 7s: Princess Diana, Steven Hawking, Leonardo DiCaprio

The number 7 imbibes the energy of Neptune, the planet of wisdom, spirituality, intuition, and higher knowledge. 7s are logical and honest. They're immersive thinkers who love to unravel the mysteries of life and death. They are fun to be around, approachable, caring, forgiving, and sympathetic, and they love to be alone. They are aware of their sophisticated nature and reject that which is without meaning or depth.

The strongest periods for 7s are June and July. Less favorable periods are January and February.

Neptune rules the glands and blood, so 7s may have stomach and dietary problems as well as inflammation of the pancreas and spleen, glandular imbalances, infections, and gout.

Those with life path 7 need to work on their mood, since they can be secretive, unassertive, and too easily hurt. People who are missing 7 from their soul code must learn lessons of intellectual and spiritual development and analyze life on deeper levels.

Life path 8: assertive, responsible, and determined
Influence of number 8: ambition
Famous number 8s: Pablo Picasso, Elizabeth Taylor, Penelope Cruz

Number 8 follows the energy of Saturn, the planet of karma; 8s are goal oriented, driven, motivated, and able to manifest success in the material world. But they also relish in having power and being in control, both over their circumstances and others.

As leaders, they are good at supervising, managing, and making money. Those with a life path 8 are attractive, caring, suave, brave, firm, independent, and romantic. They're inclined to dream and are just as talented in the arts and music as they are in finance and logistics.

Strong periods for 8s are September, October, January, and February. Weak periods are December, March, and April. Saturn is linked to the legs, so 8s are prone to rheumatism and paralysis, and, furthermore, deafness and asthma. They can also suffer from sicknesses such as indigestion, high blood pressure, and ulcers.

On the negative side, 8s are quick to get angry, easily become jealous, and have a hard time relaxing. Those missing 8 from their soul code should learn how to negotiate, handle power, supervise situations, gain authority, achieve success, invest, and earn money.

Life path 9: balanced, humanitarian, and aware
Influence of number 9: empathy
Famous number 9s: Mahatma Gandhi, Whitney Houston, Elvis Presley

Last but certainly not least is 9, which is overseen by Mars and Pluto. This number exudes the energy of idealism, humanitarianism, altruism, unfaltering generosity, and sacrifice. 9s have a divine purpose and embrace their higher mission; seldom will you meet a 9 who doesn't know why he's here. Because they have the energy of Pluto, the planet of destruction, many 9s endure sorrow, illness, and loss, which rarely breaks them down but oftentimes strengthens their grip on life. For the most part, they're calm, clever, confident, and optimistic. 9s love sports, have a good memory, and are loyal, honest, and talkative.

For 9s, strong periods are mid-March to mid-April, late October, and November. Weak periods are early March, May, June, and the beginning of October.

Mars rules the muscular system and bone marrow, while Pluto manages the immune system; thus, 9s may have respiratory, digestive, and emotional problems, as well as various infections and atrophy of their bones or muscles.

9s can be overly critical, compulsive, and sometimes traumatized, internalizing their feelings without a healthful outlet. People who don't have 9 in their soul code need to learn lessons of universal brotherhood, compassion, utopian ideals, humanitarianism, and working toward the greater good to deliver hope and peace into the world.

Refer to the appendix at the back of this book for a quick reference to the life path numbers.

HOW TO INTERPRET YOUR LIFE PATH NUMBER

As a rule of thumb, your missing numbers establish the barriers you'll have to break through and the tests you'll have to pass throughout life. Let's take Daniel, whose birthday is January 3, 1970. His primary number is 3 (1 + 3 + 1 + 9 + 7 + 0 = 21; 2 + 1 = 3). This number corresponds to Jupiter, the planet of courage, power, hard work, energy, and communication. It's a lucky planet with a powerful form of energy. Daniel, like others who have a 3 life path, is active, ambitious, extroverted, and superficial.

In Daniel's date of birth, there are two 1s, a 3, a 7, and a 9. If we add up the numbers in his year of birth, we get 8. Adding up the month, the day, and the year of his birth—separately or together—does not yield any 2s, 4s, 5s, or 6s.

Because the moon represents the mother figure, missing the 2 from his code means that Daniel may have lost his mother early on in life or that he's meant to learn significant lessons from his relationship with his mother as well as his wife or lover. One of his life challenges is to identify and resolve the karma with his mother and daughter. In real life, Daniel's mother was domineering, trying to control her son's every move, which adversely affected Daniel's relationship with women. But Daniel is aware of this and is motivated to change that in his relationship with his daughter. Here, again, is the theory that our numbers prearrange the experiences that ultimately shape our mindset.

In missing 4, the planet Uranus, Daniel must work harder than usual to achieve material order, grounding, and financial stability. He also needs to project a better image of himself at work and attract more money. Daniel has been stuck in a dead-end job for a number of years and wants to move to a different company that will recognize his talents. This is a second spiritual assignment that Daniel acknowledges and is in the process of completing.

Without 5, the planet Mercury, Daniel lacks the male energy of freedom and independence. Throughout his life, he was estranged from his father and had difficulty freeing himself from the entrapment of a controlling mother. This was perhaps his hardest lesson, since he could not attract a father figure to complement the energy of 5.

Missing 6, the planet Venus, brings the challenge of learning how to commit to a relationship and build love with a partner. In Daniel's case, he did not find a spouse or have children until later in life. His had to overcome a major impediment in order to build happiness and stability in his marriage and remain dedicated to his family.

Other numbers besides our life path determine who you are. Just as in astrology, where the characteristics of your sun sign might sometimes be overshadowed by the characteristics of a rising planet in your chart, your numerology can be influenced by numbers in your soul code other than your pure number. For example, having an 11 in your code may make you vibrate at a higher frequency than most and bestow you with the potential to be a visionary leader.

The primary number of your soul code can also be overshadowed by the day, the year, and the month of your birth, usually in that order. In most cases, the code of the day you were born on is more significant than the code of the month. Let's say that you were born on the first day of May. Your day and month are 1 and 5, respectively. The 5 that is your month is the reason your father is absent from your life, but the 1 that is your day gives you a supplemental male figure in the form of a stepfather, adoptive father, uncle, neighbor, or family friend who cared for you as a child. Because of the prominent influence of your day of birth, it can override other elements in your code that contradict its energy.

THE MEANING OF REPEATING NUMBERS

Numbers that repeat in your birthday have a particularly strong impression on you. If David was born on September 8, 1953, he has a soul code of 8 and another 8 in his day of birth. He also has a 9 in his month of birth and a 9 in his year of birth (1 + 9 + 5 + 3 = 18, 1 + 8 = 9). Number 9 is the most spiritually evolved number, and it shows that David is an old soul, having had multiple past lives. The energy of two 9s overpowers the energy of the two 8s in David's code, but the 8 life path helps David rethink his talents and purpose. Because he has only 8s and 9s in his code, David is missing many numbers and will have to undergo ample lessons in this lifetime.

Repeating numbers reinforce certain themes in your life, but it depends on the other numbers present in your code. Benjamin Franklin had a 5 both in his soul code and year of birth. Because 5s stand for independence and freedom, it's no surprise that Franklin drafted the Declaration of Independence and traveled to Paris as America's first foreign ambassador to France. The double 5 in his code made him a man of broad pursuits who cherished personal liberties.

MASTER NUMBERS

Master numbers share the same traits as their single-digit counterparts (that is to say, 2 instead of 11, 4 instead of 22, and so on.), but they act on a larger scale; they have opportunities to reach more people than single-digit life paths. Some numerologists argue that if the numbers in your birthday add up to an 11, 22, 33, or 44, you shouldn't reduce them to a single digit because they are master numbers that denote you're destined to live an extraordinary life. This is the case *only* if the month and day of your birth add up to the first master number, and the year of your birth adds up to the second master number.

Let's look at two example of true master numbers:

Amy was born on March 7, 1990, or 3/7/1990.

3 + 7 and 1+9+9+0
V V
10 19
1+0 and 1+9
V V
1 10
1 and 1+0
| V
1 1

Amy is a master number 11.

Ronald was born on February 9, 1982, or 2/9/1982.

2 + 9 and 1+9+8+2
V V
11 20
1+1 and 2+0
V V
2 20
2 and 2+0
| V
2 2

Ronald is another true master number, in his case 22.

Life path 11s desire to serve humanity to bring peace and reconciliation. They are visionaries and leaders. Famous politicians and religious figures are sometimes 11s. They display the same characteristics as 2s, but they see the bigger picture and take into account the needs of the masses.

Life path 22s are logical and pragmatic but have greater odds for success than most. They wish to share their goals with others and build something truly larger than life. They follow the same course as 4s, but they do whatever is necessary to bring the plans in their mind to reality.

Life path 33s are deeply intuitive and have an irresistible urge to teach. The person with a 33 code offers tremendous comfort to those around them; they are like a soothing balm of care and protection. This is because 33s are gifted with an almost superhuman amount of compassion and consideration. They share many attributes with 6s, but their supply of nurturing energy is endless.

Life path 44s recognize the need to cultivate their soul's calling beyond the physical sense. Theirs is a mission to heal and repair others from the inside out. Life path 44s are supremely organized and skillful in most careers, though many choose to become doctors, surgeons, and healers. They share the same description as 8s, but they possess material as well as spiritual wealth in addition to material stability.

True master numbers occur when the month and day of your birth add up to the first master digit, and the year of your birth adds up to the second master digit. Otherwise, if the month, day, and year of your birth collectively amount to a master number, you should reduce it to a single digit. Not being a master number doesn't make you any less great—it just makes you *you*!

ALL OF LIFE IS CYCLES

The higher realm shepherds us through life through the notion of time. It holds up a hand when we should wait, and points us forward when we should act. As I like to say: timing is everything, and everything in time. The more we understand time, the more we can work with it instead of fighting against it. When we try to do things in the wrong time, it can feel like walking against a strong headwind. But when we act in intervals that are supported by the universe, the wind is behind us, pushing us forward.

Like the tides of the ocean, time comes in cycles. There are cycles in which you should act and cycles in which you should wait; cycles in which you should plan and cycles in which you should build; cycles in which to begin things and cycles in which to end things. At any given moment, you are under the influence of numbers that are conducive to particular actions and not others. Personal years run in cycles of 9, and your personal year changes every year around your birthday as you enter the next year from 1 to 9. When your personal year shifts, so do the opportunities, obstacles, people, and overall energy of your life.

To calculate your personal year, add the number of your birth month and birth date to the year you want to examine. If you were born on April 23 and you want to see what personal year you're entering in 2023, you would add 4 + 2 + 3 + 2 + 0 + 2 + 3 = 16, then 1 + 6 = 7, which is a prime year for introspection and awakening. Each personal year holds a specific meaning.

Personal year 1. This is a cardinal year because in personal year 1, you control your destiny more so than on any other occasion in your life. In this year, you are setting a course that will decide whether you will be happy or unhappy, successful or unsuccessful, in a relationship or single, over the next nine years. Whatever you plan this year will endure and have longevity. It is a time during which you will find it easier to summon your inner strength. Most importantly, this is the year to plant the seeds for the projects that are dearest to you, since they have the greatest chance of blossoming and bearing fruit. If you plant nothing now and wait until a year later, you will not yield the best possible crop. This is the most advantageous year to marry, begin a business, and start making major life changes, such as buying a home or making a significant geographical move.

Personal year 2. The second personal year is a time of delays and disappointments. In this year, the forces of the universe block your energy, thwarting even the most-well-constructed plans. The key to making it through this year is patience and acceptance. It is possible to lose something important to you during a year 2. It might be a friendship that goes sour or an opportunity that slips out of your hands. Despite these setbacks, personal year 2 is an excellent year for reconciliation in relationships. If you have been unable to make peace with someone, try to do so in this year. This is a period of germination and gestation, a slow-moving year that is favorable for planting seeds of love and new romance. Getting married in your personal year 2 is a good idea, although personal year 1 is the best time.

Personal year 3. This is a year of opportunities and pleasures. The accent is on beauty, harmony, and enjoyment. If you would like to end a relationship, this is the time to do so. If you marry during this time, you will be going against the energy of the year. Personal year 3 is generally a good year for generating income and saving money, but ill-fitted for investments. For example, you might add a savings account to an account you already have, to deposit extra money, but this would not be a good time to invest that extra money in a business. It would be wiser to sell items you no longer need and to accumulate material wealth rather than begin any financial ventures. This is also a great year for meeting people. Those you welcome into your life this year will encourage and enrich you. If possible, however, avoid entering into major commitments or intense friendships in this year. Projects started in personal year 3 are fated to be short lived. If you marry, open a business, or undertake a major task, such as quitting smoking or taking up a diet-and-exercise routine, you'll find yourself in a difficult struggle.

Personal year 4. Unlike the previous year, this is a year to nurture the plans you made in personal year 1 and watch your projects grow. It is an exceptional year to initiate a new relationship and work out old family problems. New friendships made in personal year 4 will be deep and long lasting, but endings to relationships will be problematic this year. If you divorce your spouse or leave your church or social group, the situation may turn rancorous. While beginnings involving family and relationships will work out well this year, other big changes will not. The universe will not back speculative investments or sudden job shifts. Because 4 and 8 are numbers of karma, personal year 4 is a year of facing the consequences of one's actions from the past. Personal year 4 is a time to step back and look at your life. Use this year to improve your home and your health, but without making major changes, such as buying a house or switching careers. Instead, work on self-discipline and overall organization.

Personal year 5. This is the year of change, a time that brings freedom from problems alongside opportunities to improve your life. Personal year 5 is a vacation period, a perfect time to travel and focus your mind on higher matters and ideals instead of being caught up in mundane, everyday trivialities. This is not the time to start a new business. Instead, year 5 has a vibration of fertility and pregnancy, and it's easiest to get pregnant in year 5. Your finances may fluctuate in this year, but overall they should remain steady. You can use the energy of this year to your advantage by keeping your mind open to new ways of doing things and expanding on endeavors you already have underway. This year is also indicated for advertising, promotion, and fine-tuning what already exists in your life.

Personal year 6. This is the most pleasant of all years. It is a period of success. This is a year free of financial problems and a time to make adjustments to your work and come up with new ideas. You can also let go of projects that are not working for you during this time. Personal year 6 brings divine reinforcement. It has a domestic and positive vibration. This is a promising year for strengthening your relationship with your spouse and children and making improvements in your home. The energy of 6 supports your commitment to your family and sacred space. This is also a good year for healing wounds and making peace with your enemies. The vibration of personal year 6 is fortunate for the arts and for serving others. It is a time to thrive in all senses of the word.

Personal year 7. The Bible says that God created the world in six days and that on the seventh day, God rested. Similarly, personal year 7 is a time for you to rest and plan what you want to manifest in the upcoming personal year. This is a year of patience and waiting. Do not invest or plant the seeds for your future. Instead, meditate, travel, introspect, and examine the mistakes of the past so they don't repeat in future years. This is an occasion for solitude, peace, and wisdom. Do not force any issues or lose control; even if you do get your way, it will prove not to be in your favor. Avoid making any major moves this year and, if possible, stay in your home and at your current job.

Personal year 8. This is the year of karma, and the karmic impact can be felt twice as hard as in personal year 4 and when it comes to dealing with the fallout of past actions. Personal year 8 is a year of achievements and accomplishments, a time when you reap the material rewards of your efforts. Money will come from unexpected sources, and you will be presented with opportunities and recognition. It is an excellent time to look for a better job or embark on a new career altogether. This is a year for material prosperity, so ventures begun this year can work out well, especially if you begin them in the first six months of the year, when the energy of the year is strongest.

Personal year 9. Personal year 9 is a time to finish projects you have begun and a time to resolve your karma if you did not do so in personal year 8. It is a year in which to let go of things and not to begin them. This is not a year to marry or produce a child. If you separate from your partner this year, reconciliation is highly unlikely. This is also the year to drop relationships and projects that have drained you during the past life cycle of nine years. It's a good time to study, write, and plan events for the next year. It is a period for getting your affairs in order and cleaning up after the harvest of personal year 8.

THE FOUR GREAT PINNACLES

In addition to personal years, we pass through pinnacles as well. The pinnacles are four stages of life summarized by major changes and mental shifts; they are fundamental turning points that offer you the opportunity to rearrange elements in your life. You may find yourself standing at the crossroads during the transition of one pinnacle into the next. Recognizing them can give you a glimpse into what lies ahead, or what you've left unresolved, and prepare you to fix what's broken. In addition, each pinnacle is assigned a number from 1 to 9 on the basis of your birthday. The first and fourth pinnacles last 30 years, and the second and third pinnacles last about nine years. Each pinnacle epitomizes a unique form of transformation:

Pinnacle 1. The first pinnacle concerns soul-searching and development. During this time, you explore questions about your personal existence, inner world, and spiritual growth. The first pinnacle ranges from birth to approximately age 30, depending on your soul code.

Pinnacle 2. The second pinnacle stretches from the age of 30 through 39. This is when you identify your larger purpose in life and begin to find your social responsibility. This pinnacle intensifies a need to become grounded, from finding a spouse and starting a family to forming a solid career.

Pinnacle 3. The third pinnacle lasts between ages 40 and 49. This is a time for increasing your personal power and gaining true financial stability. During this pinnacle, you typically work on advancing your career and succeeding materially as well as securing a legacy for future generations.

Pinnacle 4. The fourth pinnacle debuts at age 50 and spans throughout the next 30 years. During this time, you learn to maintain balance between work and leisure, between caring for others and caring for yourself. Work starts to take a back seat to self-care during this pinnacle, and life slows down.

The progression from one pinnacle to the next, from one stage of evolution to another, is strongly felt, specifically between the first and second. The first stage of expansion is when you discover the crux of who you are. The second stage is when you put yourself in motion to achieve your purpose and passion. It's a big shift from being in your own world to projecting yourself in the outside world. As this shift occurs, you feel more responsible for what you are creating and the impact it has on others and the world.

As we know, every number carries a distinct energy. Each of the four pinnacles is given a number that is decided by your birthday. To determine the number of your first pinnacle, add the month of your birth to the day and reduce it to a single number. For March 25, for example, the first pinnacle is governed by the energy of 1 (3 + 2 + 5 = 10; 1 + 0 = 1). Knowing the meaning of 1, we know that the first pinnacle for the person born on March 25 symbolizes a great time for new beginnings.

To determine the numbers of your second pinnacle, add together your day and year of birth reduce it to a single digit. Using the same example of March 25, 1955, the second pinnacle is 9 (2 + 5 + 1 + 9 + 5 + 5 = 27; 2 + 7 = 9). We can deduce that the second pinnacle marks the end of a cycle for the person with this birthday.

To determine the numbers of your third pinnacle, add the first pinnacle to the second pinnacle. For the example above, the first pinnacle is 1 and the second pinnacle is 9, resulting in the third pinnacle being a 1 (1 + 9 = 10; 1 + 0 = 1). Therefore, the person born on March 25, 1955, has a new opportunity to "restart" his or her life during the third pinnacle. Perhaps they'll get remarried or change the course of their career.

To determine the numbers of your fourth pinnacle, add only your birth month and year (not day) and reduce it to a single digit. For March 25, 1955, the fourth pinnacle is 5 (3 + 1 + 9 + 5 + 5 = 23; 2 + 3 = 5). This means he or she will have to go through a separation or loss during this last pinnacle.

Once you have calculated the number for each pinnacle, use the following guide to find out what themes it indicates for your pinnacle:

- the time in your life when you try to attain independence
- the time of union, partnership, and cooperation; the time of emotional expression, creativity, and earning an income
- the time to build a home; a period of discipline and responsibility
- the time of change, adaptation, and freedom
- the time for love, marriage, family, and children; the time of balance
- the time for study, research, and assimilating principles of life
- the time to manage prosperity, career, and success
- the time to learn tolerance and compassion; the time to lift others and yourself; the time of maturity.

As you go through life, it's important to recognize the lessons you're being exposed to. Are you trying to gain independence or settle down in a marriage and have a family? Do you want to concentrate on kindness and empathy or focus on your career and money? When you become aware of your pinnacle's resounding theme, you can focus your attention on what you're meant to achieve in that frame of time. For example, if the period is favorable for discipline and responsibility, which is pinnacle 2, you can apply yourself to developing the abilities and skills needed to purchase a home or invest in a property.

Transitioning from pinnacle to pinnacle can be a bit chaotic, especially if you haven't finished the work you were meant to do during that period of time. The energy of your life is shifting, which means that old doors are closing (sometimes abruptly) and new ones are opening. This can feel incredibly frustrating if you don't understand why you're suddenly facing a dead end in one aspect of life, or why something you've worked hard to achieve isn't coming to fruition. Trust that the new pinnacle you're entering will bring you brand-new opportunities, perhaps better than you've had until now. Once you glean the meaning of each pinnacle and accept the divine timing of your life, you can anticipate the miracles a new chapter will deliver.

Refer to the appendix at the back of this book for a quick reference to the personal years and pinnacles.

CHAPTER TWO

CHOOSING TO VIBRATE HIGHER

Excellence is never an accident.
It is always the result of high
intention, sincere effort, and
intelligent execution; it represents
the wise choice of many
alternatives.

—Aristotle

BEFORE WE CAN LEARN MORE ABOUT NUMBERS OR ARCHETYPES, we must understand the impact that our emotions have on our personalities and relationships with others. Life is a tug of war between our strengths and our weaknesses, and each day puts us to the test. Which will we choose in response, aggression, or acceptance? As it turns out, the emotions with which we respond to everyday dilemmas set the level at which we vibrate. It's easy to lose our power and operate at low frequencies when circumstances become overwhelming. Death, illness, separation, financial problems, arguments—any of these things can rob us of our personal power. It can happen to any of the life paths, to the strongest individuals, but if we allow helplessness to overtake us, we forfeit our power to our problems and grant them control over us. After that happens, it becomes difficult to get back into position and regain our strength. Falling victim to our circumstances means that we become blind to our purpose. This is when we unknowingly vibrate lower, when it's easiest to become a "bad" person because of the bag things happening to us. We must remain conscious of how we're behaving on a day-by-day basis so as not to slip into the emotional nadirs of our numbers.

Within you lies a dormant power that begs to be awakened, indifferent to your code or archetype. Your true force can't be activated until it's been thoroughly tested: *the more you overcome, the stronger you become*. Some people think that they're weak or damaged because they've been through a lot. As a person who's been through a lot in her own life, I can assure you the opposite is true: the more challenges you defeat, the more you reinforce your willpower and build immunity against your problems. It's much easier to lose our power than to gain it, but there are many ways to revive your inherent strength. Whether they're 2s or 5s, 8s or 9s, the individuals who have discovered their inner force are the ones whose names we pronounce every day as the great thinkers and doers of this world.

THE IMPORTANCE OF YOUR FOUR EMOTIONS

Emotions add color to our world. They paint the portrait of a truly vibrant life, allowing us to feel our encounters with the world around us without restraint. Without the arousal of our sentiments, we would be stuck on a carousel of monotony, going about the motions with no real motivation or purpose. It is emotions that make us remember a single moment as the happiest of our lives or find strength within our biggest challenges. As much as they should be encouraged, emotions must also be balanced by reason. Leaning too far to either extreme—logic or feelings—will cause us to make decisions that are irrational, egoistic, or deleterious in nature. As we will see, each number or archetype is prone to certain emotions, and some do drift toward one side or the other (the Hopeless Romantic can be too emotional, the Realist can be too pragmatic, etc.).

Psychology recognizes several major emotions. Some experts believe there are five, some believe there are six. From my experience with countless individuals, I've constituted that there are four. These four emotions branch off into dozens of subsets. In fact, in 2021, researchers at University of California, Berkeley, identified 27 distinct emotions involved in reporting reliable feelings. For the most part, we are inhabited throughout the day by either anger, fear, sorrow, or love. Thinking back to our primordial beginnings, emotions were instrumental to our survival mechanisms. We relied on the keenness of our "fight-or-flight" response to recognize threats and ward off predators, usually within a second's notice. We may have evolved emotionally since then, but our emotions remain rooted within these four, with each impacting our state of mind and actions.

Our first emotion is anger. We feel angry more often than we'd like to acknowledge. Even an absent-minded driver on the road can incite rage within us. Anger raises our temperature and our blood pressure, putting extra strain on our bodies. Anger also increases adrenaline levels, which momentarily produces somewhat of a high. This explains why we love fast theme park rides and horror movies. At the peak of an anger-induced adrenaline rush, we can make irreparable mistakes: scream at our partner, fight with our friends, punch through a wall, even murder someone! Consider how most unpremeditated homicides occur: a person becomes angry (or experiences an emotional subset of anger, such as jealousy or rage), their adrenaline levels explode, and, without thinking, he grabs the first object in sight and attacks someone. But the adrenaline rush fades quickly, leaving the angry person to ask, "What have I done?" Anger is a contagious emotion, meaning that one's anger spreads to others and puts them in an irate mood too.

Hatred and anger are sibling emotions. When you hate something, you're angry at it, and vice versa. But hatred lingers in our system much longer than anger does. Anger is characterized by a peak of the emotion followed by a crash. But hatred can dwell in the subconscious mind for many years, even a lifetime. You may not be angry with your friend anymore because she stole your boyfriend many years ago, but the hatred against her remains, deep within you, and it can rear its ugly head at any moment. It is pivotal to heal yourself of both anger and hatred, for no one's sake but your own.

Our second basic emotion is fear. Fear is our most pervasive emotion and is responsible for holding us back from reaching the true potential of our lift path. When we fear something, we subconsciously build a wall against it. If you're afraid that you can't find a better job, you mentally block yourself from finding one (fear wouldn't even allow you to search for a new job in the first place). Fear restricts our creative nature and narrows our field of possibilities. Fear allows those who are in power to remain in power, because we're afraid of standing up for ourselves against those we perceive to be more powerful than us. Indeed, fear makes the weaknesses of our archetype more pronounced.

Next comes sorrow. Sorrow, or sadness, is the emotion that, if experienced frequently, leads to depression. Sorrow can range in intensity. It can vary from the absence of emotion, an empty feeling that suggests something is missing, to being filled with unbearable agony that brings on physical pain. Sadness arises when we live in the past, when we cannot make peace with what has happened and we continually revert to it in our minds. It can feel like an uncomfortable sense of melancholy or unfulfillment that won't go away. It can be difficult to pinpoint the sources of our sorrow, since there may be more than one. Usually we know why we're angry or afraid, but not always why we're sad; the answer may go back several decades to repressed trauma. Sorrow also makes us feel lost and intensifies feelings of hopelessness. Depression is a mood disorder that causes a persistent feeling of sadness and loss of interest. People who have plenty to feel happy about can become depressed, from moms with healthy kids, to teens who get everything they ask for, to CEOs of successful companies. Truly, sorrow reaches beyond an individual's circumstances and encompasses him as a whole. The problem with these first three emotions is that they feed off each other: anger invokes fear, and fear provokes sorrow. This is why many people become stuck in a cycle of negative emotions, bouncing between being angry at themselves and others, fearful about what tomorrow might bring, and saddened by their general reality.

Love is your fourth great emotion, and it is the only emotion capable of conquering the other three. It is the feeling that possesses the most healing qualities. When we're shown love, we are automatically soothed and relieved. Have you ever noticed that your pet comes to comfort you when you're down? That's because animals possess a sixth sense that they use to detect their owner's emotions. They can feel when we're stressed or sick, and try to offer us comfort. Unconditional love never fails to pick us up both emotionally and physically. Studies have demonstrated that a person in the hospital healing from an injury will heal significantly quicker if his loved ones are present versus if he is left to deal with the recovery on his own. We should spread love to others despite what they may or may not feel for us. This is hard to do because we are often shown emotions other than love. But responding with love guarantees that we heal our karma and vibrate as highly as possible for our life path.

ADDICTED TO EMOTIONS?

Can you become addicted to your emotions—dependent on feeling a certain way each day? Can a 1 life path become contemptuous toward those around him or a 2 life path enter an insidious pattern of distrust? The answer is yes. As we'll soon learn, every primary number is susceptible to specific emotions. This tendency can grow worse if that life path experiences *only* one type of emotion and enters a loop of negative feelings. Studies prove that people who have been exposed to intense negativity early on in life may develop addictions to negative behaviors as adults, ironically depending on them for emotional comfort.

By definition, an addiction is "the state of being compulsively committed to a habit or practice or to something that is psychologically or physically habit forming, such as narcotics, to such an extent that its cessation causes severe trauma." Addictions come about as a way to relieve discomfort; a person might drink himself to sleep every night to forget about his worries or stressors. In the case of emotions, the response is a neurological pattern that releases strong feelings. Those who are obsessed with "feeling a certain way" end up living at the mercy of their emotions, unable to make sensible decisions when they need to most.

Emotions can turn into addictions because of the chemistry of your brain. Within your brain exist nerve cells that are reaching out to other nerve cells at every moment of the day. Over time, these nerve cells establish an alliance. In essence, they become friends. One group of nerve cells might form a net on one side of your brain, while a different group of nerve cells may simultaneously connect on the other side of your brain—like two separate parties going on in the same house. The distinct groups stick together, much like friends at a party do. Each cluster of nerve cells represents one emotion. Take the concept of love, which is one of your four great emotions. Your notion of love is made up of the many encounters you've had with it. But it's impossible to disassociate your other emotions from the nerve cell group that represents love. The nerve cells in the group called "love" may have some nerve cells from other groups, including "disappointment," "sorrow," "hurt," and "pain," depending on your history. If you associate love with being hurt by a former partner, then "love" and "hurt" will intermingle in the same group of nerve cells.

The brain sorts every emotion and stores it into the appropriate group of nerve cells. The more it experiences one type of emotion, the more that group of nerve cells grows; more attendees turn up for the party. Ideally, we would encourage the nerve cell group called "love" to grow, but the truth is that for most of us, the groups called "anger," "hatred," and "fear" become more sizable each day. The worst part is that we become used to operating on these emotions: if you're frustrated all the time, your brain is literally prepared to receive more and more "frustrated" nerve cells. It anticipates daily emotions and produces those nerve cells in preparation. This becomes a vicious cycle, until you find yourself asking, "Since when did I become so irritated over every little thing?" By then, the neural connections are already well formed. Those tiny neurons can cause more trouble than we can imagine! It's like how a person who has an eating disorder can't break out of that eating disorder because it's become a daily habit, or how someone who's addicted to gambling swears his next hand will win the house. The mechanisms of the human brain hold true for any habit we adopt: the more we do something, the more our brain promotes that action. It gets used to anything, good or bad, sometimes supporting behaviors that are harmful to us. Our emotions, too, can become addictions, so much so that I believe they are the most-undetected forms of addiction in today's world. Only if we make mindful efforts to mitigate our feelings can we pacify their effects on our lives and archetypes.

MORE THAN FEELINGS

A life path is the manifestation of a series of strengths, weaknesses, inclinations, capabilities, predispositions. All these traits are conveyed by your emotions, so that what you feel turns us into who you are. And if you're constantly feeling and acting on low or harmful emotions, you'll erect unnecessary obstacles for yourself.

More so, what you feel translates into *how* you feel. Your emotions are an indispensable factor in your overall health. Being emotionally burdened can beget illness and disease. To achieve health on all levels and function optimally, you must first stabilize your thoughts and master your emotions.

Your mind controls every element of your being: it's the brains of the operation (literally!). You can cope with physical pain if your mind helps you see beyond the pain: if you have a broken leg, you understand the fact that it's only temporary and that it will heal. But how do you cope with a mind that's in chaos? When you're encumbered by stress, anxiety, and worry, your brain's ability to reason shuts down. Heavy mental and emotional loads are more difficult to moderate than physical ailments. There's also a logical aspect to it: if you respond to a problem with anxiety, panic, and confusion, you won't be able to figure out a solution. You won't be able to see beyond the challenge and glimpse the greater meaning. You will exacerbate the problem in the real world because you won't be able to make effective and efficient decisions.

Now more than ever, we are experiencing feelings of depression, anxiety, and isolation. The disharmony within so many people leads us to ask this: What exactly is missing from our lives that is making us so turbulent and troubled? What's missing varies for each of us. Maybe you're missing a family member whose absence left a gaping hole in your heart that turned into depression. Maybe you suffered a trauma in the past that's buried deep in your subconscious mind and resurfaces in the form of panic attacks. Maybe you've been mistreated or betrayed so many times that as a defense mechanism, you isolated yourself from others and can't seem to trust anyone.

Any of these factors might be what's missing, but the one thing that's present in every person with a mental or emotional imbalance is fear. Fear ushers irrationality. It brews darkness in our hearts and stifles our spirit. It creates racing thoughts that tell us something is definitely going to go wrong. Fear slows down our drive and switches off our motivation to live. Fear must be silenced, or it will speak volumes in our actions.

EMOTIONS, MANIFESTED

Your body reacts relative to your emotional state: if you're sad, you cry; if you're happy, you smile. But your body is doing much more to externalize what you're feeling. It's producing hormones to "match" your emotions. As we'll see, the mind-body connection becomes undeniable; certain diseases such as cancer, autoimmune disorders, depression, diabetes, and others may very well originate from the emotions you harbor within. In the scheme of numerology, your emotions push you to act in one way or another, impacting your destiny and relationships with others.

Your body responds to every emotion you experience by creating a corresponding hormone or chemical. Positive emotions result in the creation of "feel-good" hormones, while negative emotions trigger the body to produce dangerous chemicals. These chemicals invade your very cells and disrupt homeostasis (the state of equilibrium). Your cells are reproducing at every second, and what's contained within them reproduces and spreads as well.

Your emotions manifest deep inside you at the cellular level. The hypothalamus is the part of your brain that's responsible for producing chemicals; namely, neurohormones. The hypothalamus produces a neurohormone to supplement every emotion: there is a neurohormone for love, one for bitterness, one for disgust, even one for attraction!

When you begin to feel a certain emotion, a part of the pituitary gland sends out its corresponding chemical into the bloodstream, and the chemical starts to travel through your body. Cells have receptors that welcome in these chemicals. So, if you hate someone, your cells are literally filling up with a "hate" chemical.

Emotion-generated chemicals affect the normal processes taking place inside cells. The cells respond accordingly to what they receive. If "hate" chemicals are invading your cells because this is your dominant emotion, your cells will feel the effects. As you can imagine, negative emotion-generated chemicals within your cells can cause serious damage.

Cellular damage can result in mutant cells. It's not only my personal theory but the theory of many medical experts that cancer can originate by the way of harmful chemicals entering your cells and altering their functions. Remember that it takes only one mutant cell to bypass the body's checkpoints and produce a chain of mutant cells. This is why emotional balance is vital to wellness: the more your emotions are in a state of harmony, the more your body will reflect harmony. The more you will be free to make sound decisions that aren't dependent on emotions, but on awareness of yourself and those around you.

You don't have to be a victim to what you feel, dragged down by heavy emotions and stuck within self-limiting mental states. You can break free of the cycle of negative emotions and rewire the nerve cells in your brain. The most effective way to do this is the stop, examine, replace method. You should first cut off the bad emotion as soon as it starts. If you feel yourself becoming frustrated, stop the emotion by employing the rational part of your brain. You might find it effective to remind yourself why this emotion doesn't benefit you. Maybe it's irrational and unfounded or it diminishes your power in the present. Either way, reasoning through an emotion helps you block it before it gets out of hand.

Next you should examine why you feel this way. Are you afraid that you're losing control, or worried that something bad is going to happen? Do you feel the effects of an old trauma creeping in, causing similarly harmful emotions? Analyzing the source of your emotions puts them in a different perspective: they wane in strength as you begin to understand that what you are feeling is habitual, not purposeful.

Finally, you should replace the low emotion with a higher one. Whenever you feel yourself getting carried away by a negative emotion, repeat to yourself: "I choose to surrender my [negative emotion] and replace it with [positive emotion]. I banish [negative emotion] from my heart, mind, and soul. I choose to nurture only love, abundance, health, and healing within me." You should also practice meditation techniques to recenter your mind and reconnect to the greater whole to reap positive emotions. Release the mindset of isolation and surround yourself with like-minded people; there are still many good ones out there.

The moment you become aware of the fact that you're becoming frustrated, for example, and distract yourself from this emotion, some of the nerve cells in the group called "frustration" detach from each other. If you do this enough times, the "frustration" nerve group will lose its partygoers and dwindle down to nothing. It's useful to keep an emotions diary so you can recognize your feelings and anticipate which ones might come up during the day. If we relate the theory back to the various clusters in your mind, it's like the parents coming home and breaking up the party. In this case, it is your rational mind stepping in and modifying your emotions. With a bit of self-awareness, and discipline, you can emphasize positive emotions that solidify your life path's strongest points.

THE ART OF TRANSMUTATION

Can you change your archetype? If you perform sufficient inner work, can you "become" a different life path? Not exactly. You are bound by your numbers, and you will always embody many of the qualities in your code. But you have the full freedom to vibrate at your life path's highest frequency and transmute challenging character traits into advantageous ones.

Using the ability to elevate your emotions, you can live on the most positive side of your number. It involves a bit of work with your feelings, but the rewards will be invaluable; because all things begin and end in the mind, you'll begin to notice your reality improving as your thoughts shift.

The first step is to alter your stories. We're all guilty of creating stories in our minds. The brain does this as a defense mechanism. Sometimes, however, the stories we fabricate don't match reality. In the sequence of thoughts—actions—reality, our stories write the next chapter. That's because the things we envision in our minds induce energy. And if they're negative in nature, our stories invite energy that manifests as negative situations, events, and people.

Let's say your partner isn't picking up your calls. Depending on your previous experiences with him, you might start to think he's mad at you, mad with "someone else," or in trouble. You begin to flesh out these thoughts, adding details such as what the other person looks like or even planning your imminent breakup. If you dread the outcome of something, you might concoct a story that involves the worst possible scenario so that if the worst does transpire, you'll be prepared. In reality, the only thing this does is afflict your mental health and propel more doubt and desperation. The next time you find yourself creating disadvantageous stories, stop your thoughts in their tracks. Return to the present and apply logic. Examine what's making you imagine bad things: Is it a former trauma, a tendency to be pessimistic, or an erroneous belief? Remind yourself that these things haven't happened and don't need to happen. Then, distract yourself by getting out of your head. Pick up a book, read a random article, or learn about a new topic. When you feel calmer, close your eyes and start the story again. Go through the scenes and modify them to your convenience. Alter your stories regularly to regain emotional control and project more-positive outcomes in time.

Another key to living on the positive spectrum of your number is being able to communicate your needs. Feelings that become trapped inside tend to explode sooner or later, hurting you and those around you. As we learned, they can also turn into physical diseases. Communication means being able to release how and what you feel not just to others, but to yourself. It's essential to be honest with yourself so as not to build up unrealistic expectations that lead to failure or exasperation. Facing the truth about what's happening in the present grounds you, and introspecting on what you'd like to improve puts you in charge of these changes. Don't be afraid to speak up about what's making you upset to your boss, partner, family member, or friend. You can organize your thoughts on paper before you say them out loud. Surround yourself with supportive people with whom you can share anything without feeling ashamed or unworthy. A strong support group can gift you with greater confidence and motivation, attributes of good mental health.

Even if you're in a bad situation, you can choose to turn things in your favor. But when you feel too many emotions at once, you might not know what to choose; you can't see what you have to do, because fear, impatience, or doubt is blocking your vision. Before making a decision, clear your heart and mind. Take a few deep, calming breaths and center yourself. Consider what you would advise your best friend to do if he or she were in your position.

Feel your fear leaving your body as bravery takes its place. Block out your doubts and welcome in certainty. Remove yourself from your desperation and hand it over to the universe. You might not be able to instantly change your emotions, but with practice you'll learn how to shift into love, understanding, and acceptance, more and more easily each time.

When your emotions are positive, you feel stable enough to make decisions that lead you to take new actions. They say the definition of insanity is doing the same thing over and over and expecting different results, and they're right! This can mean taking the same actions in a relationship, your workplace, or your family. If you keep doing something that results in you feeling dissatisfied, stop doing it and restrategize. You might think you have no other choice, but you do—no one decides how you should act but you! If you feel miserable in your job, don't hesitate to have a serious conversion with your boss or seek other employment. Or if your dynamic with a toxic person is harming your mental health, don't think twice to distance yourself from him or her. When you shift the way you behave, others will shift the way they react to you. In this way you transform the energy around you and, by extension, the situations you attract. Changing your course of action is the only way to reinforce a new outcome and feel more at ease on the inside.

Disconnecting from pressure has a lot to do with the emotions we choose to apply to everyday life. The truth is that your spirit is naturally tranquil; all the factors that disrupt it are external, and the pressure of the modern world is enough to drive anyone crazy. It's easy to get lost in the daily haze of work, traffic, bills, and trying to fulfill the needs of everyone else. We place a lot of emphasis on connecting to others, but disconnecting is just as important. Take time to be alone each day. You can take a drive, walk in nature, sit by a lake, meditate in your bedroom, or do whatever you most want to do on your own. Don't put off this hour of solitude; embrace it as a holy connection with your higher self. Mute your phone, skip the music, and forget about social media. Try to hear the sapient voice of silence that speaks from within: peer inside yourself and face your shadow without fear. Visualize yourself reaching your goals and allow a surge of joy to surface. Say a prayer, repeat a few affirmations, or cry if you need to. Try to pinpoint what is most affecting you and how you can improve it. With courage, conviction, and a solid self-relationship, you can resolve almost anything.

Having an attitude of gratitude goes a long way in controlling emotions and becoming your best self. Instead of fretting about things that didn't go your way, take a moment to thank the universe for the many things that did work in your favor. No matter how dispirited you may be feeling or how unfair you think life has been to you, find just one reason to be grateful right now. It can be something simple or obvious, but don't take it for granted. Then, speak your gratitude out loud. You can say things like "Thank you for keeping me safe during that accident" or "Thank you for giving me a roof over my head." Take a few moments to reflect on the positive portions of your life. Remember, there's someone in this world who would give anything to be in your place.

Your mind is the precursor to your reality. Guard it, honor it, and make it a safe haven—such actions will transmute not only your emotions, but your future.

USING WORDS TO SHIFT CIRCUMSTANCES

Affirmations are proven methods of self-improvement because of their ability to rewire the brain. Like physical exercise, they raise the level of feel-good hormones and create new clusters of "positive thought" neurons within the brain. In the sequence of thought–speech–action, affirmations play an integral role by breaking patterns of negative thoughts, negative speech, and, in turn, negative actions. What you speak and what you get go hand in hand. That's because what you think, you speak; what you speak, you do; and what you do, you become. No word is empty, because every sound you make engages energy toward or against you. For this reason, you must be careful with your words, choosing to speak only those that cultivate your highest good.

Chants, mantras, and affirmations have been around since human beings developed a system of speech. They were first used as a form of prayer, a way of asking the universe for what we needed to survive: water, food, rain, crops, and so on. Repeated phrases were woven into the cultures and traditions of tribes all over the globe before modern societies prospered. In Hinduism and Buddhism, a mantra is a sacred utterance that possesses a spiritual force behind it. Buddhists chant during meditation, and mantras are a key part of initiation ceremonies in many Hindu sects. Music evolved from chanting, which is why the verse and chorus of a song are repeated several times. Affirmations can be thought of as a form of prayer except in the present tense, as if the things we're praying for are happening right now.

Rarely do we recognize the magnitude of our words; you tell yourself things every day without paying attention to what you're affirming to be true. Out of habit, you might tell yourself, "I'm scared," "I'm tired," "I'm desperate," "I'm stuck," or "I'm not good enough." You don't realize that your words become the truth of your life. I remember growing up in Romania in a small village with no running water and envisioning myself in a completely different place at a different time. I always saw myself singing ever since I was a little girl. One day I was walking through the center of the town in which my family and I lived, when my vision suddenly changed; I no longer saw the marketplace in front of me. I saw myself grown up, wearing a gold sparkling dress and singing my heart out on stage to an audience of thousands of people. I tugged at my mother's dress and yelled out that I was going to be a famous singer. She looked at me curiously and said, "Sure you are, dear." My mother always told me I would go to school and work at the bank, like my father. Time and time again I corrected her: "No, I'm going to be a singer."

Fueled by my intuition, I spoke my dreams out loud. I affirmed my abilities and strengthened my potential to become what I knew I was destined to become. And through the right actions, I did become the famous singer I promised my parents I would be. I was able to do this because I learned about the force of the spoken word from a very young age; when someone told me "No," I said, "Yes." I recognized that affirmations release our needs into the universe. When we think something, we generate an idea, but that thought is incomplete because it's contained within our minds; it doesn't travel beyond our energy field. People often speak about the law of attraction, which states that what you think, you will become. But that theory is incomplete, because only when you speak do you send your thoughts out on a mission to manifest into reality. Visualizations are great tools for expanding our desires and shifting our perception, but they must also be accompanied by words and actions so as to change circumstances in the real world. Imagine a world in which no one spoke to each other, and we only *thought* of what we needed to do; the world would become stationary without speech, because progress relies on communication. The universe, too, needs to hear you. It needs you to declare your hopes, wishes, and goals so that it can assist you in materializing them. We can't become what we think unless we share our intentions with the Divine, and this we can accomplish through the art of self-empowering speech.

Words are composed of sounds, with each sound holding a specific resonance. The very first words of the Bible read, "In the beginning there was the word, and the word was with God, and God was the word." The Hindu Vedas begin likewise by stating that "in the beginning was Brahman with whom was the Word, and the Word is Brahman." The holy Islamic text, the Qur'an, regards creation thus: "He is the Originator of the heavens and the earth. When He decrees a thing, He only says to it 'Be' and it is." It's interesting to note that all three religious texts begin with mention of Spirit's sacred word, out of which the entire universe was formed. According to these scriptures and others, our world, wrought out of chaos, sprang from Divine speech. Perhaps this is why Hindu, Buddhist, and Jewish mystics alike believe that sound both creates and pervades matter.

Sounds are frequencies, invisible waves that travel through the air and carry energy. Even though we can't see sounds, they exist everywhere. They can contain healing qualities; in Ayurveda, or "the science of life," you can heal yourself through techniques that include sound therapy. Sound is able to break negative vibrations by shattering their energy. If you're working on your voice, you might have been encouraged to practice your vocals and consonants. When you practice them, pay attention to where the sound stops in your body; the sound will stop where there is a problem. Sound therapy can help you become aware of your body, its deficiencies, and its needs. Every letter of our alphabet carries a frequency. This is why your name reveals so much of who you are. The energies associated with your name become your dominant energies and endow you with a special force.

When you release your thoughts, your words affect not just you but the entire universe. What you speak travels through universal waves and causes a small ripple in the possibility of the future. When you say things like "I can't" or "It won't happen," you're introducing limitations to the infinite potential that lies in the future. That tiny ripple traveling through the universe meets a dead end. In comparison, when you say, "I can" or "It is happening for me," you're applying hope. Hope forges a clear path ahead for your wishful ripple.

Have you noticed that people who are positive are also more successful in life? That's because negative people deplete their energy and deprive themselves of motivation. Those who articulate positivity and declare their intentions with hope find new reasons to advance toward their goals. Positive affirmations can also greatly reduce stress, which can induce headaches, ulcers, high blood pressure, and heart disease, so we should do everything possible to reduce everyday stress. Many people find that positive affirmations work wonders for stress relief because speech is a natural channel for emotional release.

My late husband was diagnosed with stage 4 lung cancer in 2007 and passed away two years later. I will always remember when the doctors walked into his hospital room and, with the rest of his family present, told him he wouldn't make it another three months. Everyone was shocked because they believed the doctor. But my husband looked the doctor right in the eyes and told him: "Yes, I will; I'll be around for years from now." My husband lived to see the holidays that year, and the next year, and the next. He told us every year that he'd continue to live. I truly believe his affirmations helped him live a much longer life than he was expected to. The force of our words can make terrible or wonderful things happen; the choice is ours.

Words can be highly damaging to a person if misused. Physical scars close and fade over time, but emotional and mental scars from verbal abuse never heal or disappear. They remain like an open wound inside the person. You should never allow anyone to use harsh words against you—stop them before they finish the sentence! No matter how strong or confident of a person you are, a part of you will always revert back to their negative words and wonder: "Is that really true? Am I really that way?" If a mother tells her daughter, "You're not good enough for a man; you'll never get married," then she might really have trouble finding a partner. I've seen many cases like this in my career. You may or may not remember when you're told, "I love you" or "You are smart; you will succeed." But sadly, you will remember when someone says, "I hate you" or "You're so stupid." This is because hurtful words have a higher chance of becoming incorporated into our long-term memory, where they will affect future thoughts and behaviors. Bad words stored in our memory are like a doorstop: they will never allow the door to the past to close completely.

As I always say, reality reflects what the mind projects. Your thoughts translate into your speech, and your words are the seeds you plant into the earth; they are waiting to come break through the soil, to grow and flourish. And once spoken, words cannot be taken back. They roam eternally within the energy of the universe.

50 AFFIRMATIONS FOR HIGHER VIBRATIONS

Buddha once said, "Better than a thousand hollow words is one word that brings peace." You don't need to repeat a thousand affirmations each day to feel better about yourself or to change your reality. You need only a few simple and effective mantras to bring you peace and stability. Affirmations purify your thoughts and restructure the dynamic of your brain so that you start to believe that nothing is impossible. The word "affirmation" comes from the Latin *affirmare*, originally meaning "to make steady, strengthen." Affirmations strengthen you by leading you to believe in the potential of an action you want to manifest. When you verbalize your dreams and ambitions, you're instantly empowered with a deep sense of reassurance that your words will become reality. You'll be surprised to learn how much force beats within every syllable you speak.

Pick a few phrases that resonate most with you from the list that follows. You can use any of these affirmations alone or in combinations—the possibilities for empowerment are endless! Feel free to change the words so that they're tailored to your specific needs: instead of "I am resilient," for example, you can say, "I am resilient enough to overcome this breakup and find a new, loyal partner." What's most important is to establish communication with the universe. Recite these affirmations first thing in the morning and throughout the day. Pronounce them with conviction and in your own voice to make them happen in the real world. In time, these statements will roll off your tongue fluently and freely. Practicing such affirmations daily will harmonize your emotions and promote your life path to its highest potential:

I am more powerful than my pain; nothing is as great as my own power.

I have the strength to defeat any adversity; I break through barriers and leap over hurdles effortlessly.

I am in love with who I'm becoming; I give up on pleasing others and work to satisfy my highest self.

I am in control of my life; I am master over my circumstances.

I reject all that weakens me and welcome all that strengthens me.

I am worthy; I deserve the incredible things that are coming to me.

I am attracting the perfect person for me; the universe is sending me a partner who is dedicated, faithful, and unconditionally loving.

I am healthy, I am stable, I am sound; my body is whole and my mind is brilliant.

I accept my flaws and embrace the totality of who I am.

I am unstoppable; I remain undeterred from my dreams and am determined to reach my goals.

I am superior to negativity; I rise above my troubles and remain within the realm of positivity.

I am talented; I have been gifted with endless skills that I hone each day.

I am emotionally pure; a river of compassion washes away my anger and replaces it with love.

I am extremely successful; my career is growing, expanding, and thriving.

Today, I choose joy over suffering; I am content with my progress and grateful for my blessings.

I am loved; I am appreciated, admired, and respected by the people who matter most to me.

I am resilient; my ability to triumph over challenges is unfailing.

I am purposeful; I am meant to impact the world in positive and profound ways.

I am limitless; my soul is eternal and my potential is infinite.

I am fearless; I have the courage to take necessary risks that shape my future for the better.

I am beautiful; I radiate charm and grace.

I am alive right now; I choose to engage fully and deeply in this present moment.

I am full of faith; my uncertainties are replaced by conviction.

I am evolving and becoming the best version of myself; I am growing smarter, wiser, and more enlightened each day.

I make excellent choices that lead to my ultimate good.

I am irresistible to my significant other; our bond is fortified every day.

I am in sync with the universe; I am guided in my endeavors every step of the way.

I am proud of myself; I have achieved so much already and will achieve so much more.

I am all-knowing; all that I need to know, I already know, and all the guidance I need is within me.

I am liberated; my life is uncomplicated, unbound, and free to take its predestined course.

I am brimming with creativity and new ideas; I meet like-minded people and connect with the wonderful world around me.

I am reborn; my life is just beginning, and my path is carved toward greatness.

I am unafraid to say no; I stand up for myself whenever necessary and do only what I feel comfortable doing.

I am my own best friend; I can count on myself to accomplish everything I set my mind to.

I honor myself and treat myself gently; I give my body all that it needs to thrive.

I am protected; the divine watches over me at all times and I follow its voice to safety.

I am magic; I have the ability to manifest all that I envision.

I am the future; I plant the seeds for a better tomorrow in this very moment.

I am at peace with everything that has happened, is happening, and will happen.

I choose to see others with forgiving eyes; even if they have hurt me, I forgive all.

I understand the bigger reasons behind setbacks and use my challenges as fuel for my future.

I am detaching from what does not serve me; there is place only for positivity in my life.

I am on the threshold of a brand-new chapter in my life; I am met with unexpected joys and new opportunities.

Love is my birthright; I am a product of compassion and kindness.

I have full control over my fate and trust that Spirit will guide me to make great decisions.

I am overflowing with joy, vitality, and energy.

I leave my pain in the past and heal in the present; harmony blossoms within me.

I acknowledge my immense self-worth; my confidence is soaring.

My efforts are being supported by the universe; my divine destiny is unfolding before my eyes.

I am the architect of my life; I build its foundations upon hope and decorate its walls with optimism.

BALANCING YOUR CHOICES

A large part of vibrating higher comes from making smart decisions, ones that are inspired by intuition but immersed in logic. Life is a series of decisions; they are the building blocks of life. Each day, you're faced with choices that alter your health, relationships, family, and finances, often forever. That's because no choice is without impact; every decision you make—drastic or minor—will influence your future in one way or another. Even the most-minuscule choices can have a tremendous effect. One tiny decision can cause a domino effect that alters your entire life. Never underestimate the power of a single choice: one thing done differently and purposefully can bring you greater joy, stability, and peace of mind. It's critical to learn how to make the best decisions notwithstanding your archetype's tendencies.

We don't realize that on a daily basis, we make hundreds of decisions. Every action we take is weighed by our brain before we take it. Some, we may contemplate for hours (or days), such as whether we really want to marry the person to whom we're engaged. Others, we decide in a fraction of a second, such as swerving to avoid an accident when the car in front of us slams on the brakes. Ultimately, decision-making is a problem-solving activity: we make decisions in order to resolve perceived problems. They are supposed to be based on our values, beliefs, and knowledge. But more often than not, our choices arise out of fears, insecurities, and traumatic memories—all of which stem from unprocessed negative emotions. When we act on the wrong markers, our decisions may cause more problems than they solve.

Perhaps what's most interesting is how our brain activity varies on the basis of our decisions. Decision-making—as well as character, reasoning, and emotions—is controlled by the frontal lobe of the brain. This part of the brain is extremely quick acting: it predicts a decision's outcome up to 10 seconds before we're even aware that we're making a choice. A decision, therefore, is reached by our brain before we cognize it. There are instances when our decisions are made for us, such as in the case of pressure from others or when we're following instructions. Studies published in *Nature Neuroscience* have shown that if we're told what to do, less of our brain lights up, meaning we feel less confident in our choices. If we act out of free will, more of our brain lights up, meaning we feel more convinced of our decisions.

The front portion of the frontal lobe isn't fully developed until we're adults. In fact, a brain doesn't "mature" until we're nearly 30 years old. This area of the brain, also called the prefrontal cortex, handles high-level cognitive abilities such as problem-solving and planning. It also handles (you guessed it) making decisions. Until then, decisions are made by the amygdala, the part of our brain associated with emotions, impulses, aggression, and instinct. This explains why teenagers make some terrible choices—they're brains aren't fully formed yet!

In adulthood, your archetype generally designates the types of choices you make. It plays a vital role in the decisions you make throughout the day, from the time you wake up (early or late), to the way you drive to work (passively or aggressively), to the way you interact with your peers (openly or restrainedly), to the amount of effort you put into your projects (all or nothing). At home, your life path is responsible for how closely you connect with your family members and how you treat your significant other. Your emotions, which are intrinsically connected to your archetype, influence the neuroscience of decisions. For example, after an argument with his partner, the Introvert might take time to be by himself, the Hopeless Romantic might ask for forgiveness, the Well-Rounded One might suggest solutions, the Free Spirit might simply walk out, and so on. You can imagine that each of these different scenarios—these different decisions—yields different results for the relationship. These are just a few of the countless decisions determined by your archetype each and every day.

Making good decisions goes hand in hand with self-knowledge: being familiar with the propensities of your archetype will give you key insight not only into your strengths and weaknesses, but into how you can make smarter choices at every turn. You alone hold the power to make better decisions than yesterday, because the choices you are making right now are writing the script for tomorrow. Here are 16 decisions I encourage you to take today and every day:

Choose to let go of what brings pain. Before you can create your future, you must make peace with your past. This entails forgiveness. No one can hurt you if you forgive them, because forgiveness takes their power away and returns it to you. When you choose to forgive, you detach yourself from your obstacles and regain control of your decisions: you make choices based on love and acceptance instead of anger and resentment. By disengaging yourself from what brings you pain, you can make progress. Know that no matter what happened, you always have the ability to make yourself whole again, and it starts by letting go. Forgiveness shifts the course of your life by disconnecting you from harmful thoughts and behaviors. It sets you free from suffering and liberates you to encounter new joys and opportunities. Forgiveness is a decision that will help you live well this and every year to come.

Choose to create a bigger version of yourself. Often we reduce our potential without even realizing: we limit ourselves to fit a certain mold that other people have invented for us. What would your life look like if you had no restrictions? Who would you be if you didn't abide by the dictates of others? Write down the description of your bigger version. For example, you can write, "My bigger version is a business owner who just bought her first property," or "My bigger version lost 30 pounds and is happily married to her soulmate." Expand on this description little by little, filling in details that resonate with your higher self. Then, take small actions each day of the year that are in alignment with who you want to become.

Choose to keep things simple. Complications rob you of joy. Introspect on what is creating disorder in your life right now and what you can do to ease entanglements. If a relationship, friendship, or problem at work has become so convoluted that it drains you of energy, make the decision to step back and take a break from it. Then, notice how you feel once you've distanced yourself from a person or situation and simplified matters: Have your emotions become more healthful? Do you feel less frustration and more freedom? The best things in life are the simplest, and one of the smartest choices you can make is to keep them that way.

Choose to do good. Don't hesitate to take any opportunity to do good. Doing good will keep your conscience clean and clear your preordained path of blockages. Don't regret if you've been good to people who didn't deserve it; that's their karma, not yours. Performing acts of kindness and choosing to help others in small ways increases feel-good hormones in your brain and creates a sense of reward. It connects you to others more deeply and reinforces the common thread that runs throughout the human race: we're all here to love and be loved.

Choose to invest in your health. Don't wait until it's too late to make healthful decisions. Eat well, move your body, surround yourself with supportive people, take care of your mental health, and do at least one thing each day that makes you smile. All external relationships are limited and temporary, but your relationship with yourself is permanent; it lasts for the duration of your life. Choose to make it a healthful one and love yourself unconditionally. If you put yourself last at the expense of pleasing others, you will find that other people won't do it for you. Remember that you are your single greatest investment, and if you don't invest in yourself, who will?

Choose to focus on the moment. The rates of anxiety and depression are soaring across the globe as a result of our constant battle with time. Brooding over what could've been in the past and stressing about what might be in the future disrupts your mental and emotional well-being. Living outside time disempowers you; it subtracts from the force you have right now—to create, persuade, and transform. When you feel yourself fretting about the past or future, reel yourself back to the present. Close your eyes and concentrate on your surroundings: What do you smell, hear, taste, and feel? Run your hands along an object and take note of its texture, size, shape, etc. You exist here, you are powerful now, and you can choose to use the resources you have available to make the best of this moment, whatever it may be.

Choose to spend your time wisely. Time is one of the only elements of life you can't regain: you can't make up for lost time. From now on, choose your minutes, hours, and days more wisely and focus on making every moment count. This means spending less time in a virtual reality and more time in the physical one. Challenge yourself not to check social media for a day or two, and to go on a walk with your family members instead of watching a movie. Choose to take an hour out of your day to meditate, visualize your future, and write down your deepest wishes. Such examples of self-reflection are time well spent.

Choose to have a sense of humor. Life just *feels* easier when you don't take things too seriously. Problems will come and go for all of us, but those of us who choose to find the humor in things will overcome our challenges with much more ease and grace. So laugh at your problems; they are no match for you! Take a burden off your shoulders by choosing to be more lighthearted and carefree. This decision detaches you from stress and anxiety and puts you back in control.

Choose to save instead of spend. We all buy plenty of things we don't need! This applies to some archetypes more than others, such as the Extrovert and the Free Spirit. Instead of buying things online because you're bored or splurging on items simply because they're attractive, make the smart decision to save your money and invest it in things that will grow in value: tangible objects such as a property or gold and silver. Put aside a few dollars a day, or as much as you can, and watch how your decision will compensate you in time.

Choose to have faith. Faith is the belief that something greater exists. The universe wants to work with you to help you meet your goals, but you must first build a solid foundation of faith. You don't have to practice a certain religion; you simply have to hold the conviction that Spirit is within you. Establish daily rituals that secure your faith, such as saying short prayers throughout the day, lighting a candle for someone going through a hard time, or heeding intuitive knowledge that's passed down from your higher self. Choosing to have faith can light up even the darkest moments and aid you in making more-sound decisions.

Choose to follow your intuition. Take a small leap of faith and trust your intuition on one issue you're currently having. If your gut feeling is telling you something's not right in your relationship, try to get to the bottom of it. Or, if you're in between jobs and looking left and right with no luck, allow your inner insight to steer you to the right career for you. Concentrate on a decision that requires your attention. Don't hesitate and don't second-guess your intuition. Act on it and watch what happens! Intuition can be a great source of enlightenment, working hand in hand with your rational mind to help you make the best decisions.

Choose to think twice. Thinking twice is as important as going with your gut feeling. Choices should be weighed in terms of the effects they'll have on your life in the long run. Often, our emotions interfere in our decision-making process; we feel apprehensive if we don't make a choice right away or are obliged to make choices that benefit others more than us. This can disturb our inner harmony, creating restless or fearful thoughts. Starting today, make decisions based on long-term consequences, not sudden whims. Always ask yourself, "If I do this, how will it affect me in one, five, and ten years from now?" and "Does this contribute to my ultimate good?"

Choose to take nothing for granted. We don't realize how blessed we are until we lose something dear to us, whether it's a person or possession. Only in hindsight can we comprehend just how fortunate we were. Starting today, adopt an attitude of gratitude; concern yourself less with what you don't have and more with all that you do have. Focusing on your blessings opens the door for even more. That's because when you shift your thoughts to appreciation instead of dissatisfaction, you carve new neural pathways in your brain. You train yourself to think more-positive thoughts, which will inspire more-mindful decisions.

Choose to reinvent yourself. Each of us holds a unique set of beliefs that shapes our perception. Life requires constant revision, but of the deeper kind: before anything else, it's necessary to reevaluate our beliefs to make sure they're still serving our purpose. Otherwise, we can become static in our mindset and stuck in unfavorable situations. Contemplate on what you do or think that you're unhappy with, and how can you change it. Come up with new and innovative ways you can sustain yourself, express yourself, and improve yourself each day.

Choose to value community. In the Western world, we're taught to value individuality over community. While individuality increases personal power, community is the heart of overall progress. The COVID-19 pandemic reminded us of the importance of community; it reiterated the truth that at the end of the day we are all one, and that what hurts one person hurts us all. Become involved in your community in any way you can, whether it's checking up on your neighbors or volunteering at a local shelter. After all, our greatest accomplishments were never achieved alone.

Choose to create your future. Because you are the cocreator of your life, you can choose your future. Concentrate and write down five things you want to happen within the next year. For example, if you are looking for a job, close your eyes and envision your new job. What will your boss look like? What does the setting look like? How will you get this job? Then, jot it all down. You can write, "I'm working in an office with three other women. The walls are a light blue and there are many windows." Write down your predictions in the *indicative mood*, as if they're happening right now. One year later, revisit your journal and see how many of your five predictions came true.

Choosing to emanate your life path's best qualities will help you enjoy smooth and stable relationships, as we'll see in the next chapter.

CHAPTER THREE

THE NUMBERS IN LOVE

Every heart sings a song, incomplete, until another heart whispers back. Those who wish to sing always find a song. At the touch of a lover, everyone becomes a poet.

—Plato

NUMEROLOGY BECOMES EVEN MORE INTERESTING when you compare your numbers to your partner's. Here, compatibility and karma can be measured by studying the numbers both of you have in your codes, as well as the ones you're missing. Sharing numbers with your significant other shows that you have experiences, character traits, and beliefs in common and that you will face many of the same issues. If both you and your partner are born on the seventh day of the month, you share the number 7 and are likely to be fascinated by metaphysics. If you're both born in September, the ninth month, you're likely to be generous and humanitarian. But there's another element that analyzing birthdays can reveal: shared karma from past lives. As we'll learn later in this chapter, if a person's life path coincides with his partner's year of birth, the couple shares past-life karma.

Beyond the general rules of numerology, each life path can be assigned an archetype that's representative of its principal traits and ruling qualities. The word "archetype" comes from the Greek *archein*, meaning "original," and *typos*, meaning "pattern." So an archetype is an original pattern. In psychology, it's a pattern of thought present in the human psyche. Like Western numerology, archetypes have their roots in ancient Greece. The forerunner of prototypes was Plato's theory of forms, which asserts that all forms (things) on Earth draw their origins from forms in the realm of ideals. According to this theory, the patterns we perceive in our world are merely representations of a perfect pattern on some higher plane of existence.

Our personalities, too, derive from universal archetypes that are subsumed into our subconscious. Every person displays a dominant archetype, but we can show hints of other archetypes on the basis of the arrangement of numbers in our code. You may be an Extrovert if your life path is a 3, but a 2 in your day of birth might give you introverted tendencies. If you read about your life path but don't fully resonate with its description, look at what other numbers are present in your code. They may be influencing the energy of your personality.

Each of the life paths in numerology is represented by an archetype:

Life Path 1: The Independent
Life Path 2: The Introvert
Life Path 3: The Extrovert
Life Path 4: The Realist
Life Path 5: The Free Spirit
Life Path 6: The Hopeless Romantic
Life Path 7: The Spiritual Seeker
Life Path 8: The Workaholic
Life Path 9: The Well-Rounded One

We will learn how each archetype corresponds to its life path number, how his mind processes reality, and how he exerts himself in the outside world.

HOW THE NUMBERS EXPRESS EMOTIONS

Because emotions radiate from the core of our being, they act as markers for archetypes: they help distinguish the different personalities from one another, lay out the inclinations of each archetype, and set up predictable patterns of behavior. Every one of the nine numerology archetypes has dominant emotions that can hurt or help his relationships:

The Independent can hurt his relationships by being stubborn, detached, and disinterested. He can help his relationships by being receptive, responsible, and reliable.

The Introvert can hurt his relationships by being isolated, reserved, and overly analytical. He can help his relationships by being open, confident, and trusting.

The Extrovert can hurt his relationships by being superficial, gullible, and dramatic. He can help his relationships by being self-aware, optimistic, and creative.

The Realist can hurt his relationships by being close minded, undemonstrative, and insensitive. He can help his relationships by being adaptive, passionate, and intimate.

The Free Spirit can hurt his relationships by being unconventional, careless, and disoriented. He can help his relationships by being purposeful, diligent, and practical.

The Hopeless Romantic can hurt his relationships by being idealistic, reckless, and self-sacrificial. He can help his relationships by being logical, balanced, and self-loving.

The Spiritual Seeker can hurt his relationships by being philosophical, intense, and inattentive. He can help his relationships by being profound, intuitive, and considerate.

The Workaholic can hurt his relationships by being critical, greedy, and selfish. He can help his relationships by being modest, simple, and altruistic.

The Well-Rounded One can hurt his relationships by being overwhelmed, melancholic, and patronizing. He can help his relationships by being malleable, compassionate, and soft spoken.

Whether a person lives on the negative or positive side of his emotional spectrum is his decision. As we learned in the previous chapter, anyone can choose to evolve and prompt calmer, steadier emotions as opposed to hasty, aggressive ones, and each archetype can transmute what he feels by making better emotional choices day after day.

DECIPHERING PAST LIVES

Another gift that numerology gives us is the ability to detect bonds that originated in past lives, since these sorts of connections reveal themselves through birthdays. To determine inherited karma, look at your and your significant other's life paths and birth years. If your life path coincides with your love interest's year of birth, or vice versa, you share past-life karma.

A client named Helen came to me one day to ask about her connection to a new man she was dating. She stated that she felt inexplicably drawn to this person. Helen was born on May 10, 1963, so I quickly tallied up her numbers and found that her divine code was 7 (5 + 1 + 0 + 1 + 9 + 6 + 3 = 25; 2 + 5 = 7). The man she was interested in, Raul, was born on February 23, 1960, making him a life path 5. A 7 and a 5 can get along, but that wasn't what piqued my interest; what was fascinating to me was that Raul's year of birth, 1960, added up to a 7, which coincided with Mary's divine code. This was a clear indication of past lives and explained the curious intensity this new pair shared.

Another client, Colin, was in a relationship for many years with his partner, Paulo. Colin confessed that although he loved Paulo, he felt their relationship often turned intense and at times onerous, being forced to pass through trials that Colin could not comprehend. Colin was born on October 6, 1981, making him an 8 (1 + 0 + 6 + 1 + 9 + 8 + 1 = 26; 2 + 6 = 8). His birth year, 1981, summed up to a 1 (1 + 9 + 8 + 1 = 19; 1 + 9 = 10; 1 + 0 = 1). Paulo was born on August 11, 1980, which meant that his code was a 1 (8 + 1 + 1 + 1 + 9 + 8 + 0 = 28; 2 + 8 = 10; 1 + 0 = 1). Paulo's life path matched Colin's year of birth, symbolizing another past-life karma and the reason behind the ordeals the couple was being forced to endure.

This quick and simple method can unveil whether you and your other half have passed together through previous lives. If you did, your relationship is likely karmic, which we'll see is one of the seven types of relationships. First, let's look at what karma really means and how it plays out in our relationships.

SECRETS OF SHARED KARMA

Many people have a skewed perception of karma. When they hear the word, they automatically think that karma's a "you know what." While there does exist "payback" karma, the true nature of karma is much more encompassing and merciful than serving vengeance. Karma is not some malicious force that brings your bad deeds back to you; it is the first and foremost law of the universe. Karma is the reaction to every action, the memory of every one of your thoughts, intentions, and actions from this and prior lifetimes. More specifically, it is the memory of your soul, an imprint on your spiritual DNA that materializes throughout your life in the form of people you meet and things that happen to you. Your karma is attached to your being and belongs to you in the same the way your physical features belong to you.

This explains why you meet certain people to whom you feel instantly and intensely connected from the beginning, whether they're friends or lovers. We've all been struck by a sense of déjà vu before: you may have met someone and thought, "Do I know him from somewhere?" That feeling of familiarity is your distant karmic memory springing up from your subconscious. In all actuality, you may have known this person in a past life, and your souls agreed to meet once more. When we die, the division between our conscious and unconscious disappears and we reclaim all our memories of the past, including our past lives. As a soul on the other side, you perform a life review; you long to return to Earth to weave your way through another lifetime, with the intention of picking up where you left off. Your soul recognizes the human experience as an opportunity to settle issues you may not have gotten to in your last life.

I experienced déjà vu when I first met my husband. As he introduced himself and shook my hand, I almost fainted! I was blindsided by a sudden vision of us walking arm in arm hundreds of years ago in Paris. I was sure that we had known each other in a past life. We shared karma, or unfinished business, that had been transferred down to this lifetime. We were destined to meet again, start a family, and pass through joys and hardships alike, just like you were destined to meet the people you've encountered so far in your lifetime. No one crosses your path by accident.

Karma accounts for more than past-life relationships. Many of the things—good or bad—that are happening to you are not new; they're karmic episodes replaying from former lifetimes. Karma works in highly predictable ways: it carries over from prior incarnations, setting you up for the same patterns. Unresolved karma will always find a way of repeating itself. This means that similar sequences of events will take place more than once. If you were rich in a past life, money might come to you easily in this life. If you suffered from a certain illness in a past life, you're more likely to develop the same disease during this reincarnation. If someone stole from you in a past life, that person might come back and steal from you again. And if you were with a partner whom you loved deeply in a past life, you will be with that soul again, even if the odds are against you.

In your love life, unsettled karma will bring about nearly identical scenarios, such as the same kinds of relationships, until you become aware and take appropriate action. If you want to clear your love karma, you must recognize when a relationship is karmic and take appropriate action to resolve the karma that you and your partner share. If you were abandoned by your mother, you may end up abandoning your spouse instead of your child. Yet, part of you knows you have repeated your mother's behavior, only in a different way. Promising not to be like the one who harmed you is not enough. You must reconcile the old or bad karma that you carry with you, or you will manifest it in one way or another during your life. Without karma to make us feel uncomfortable, our relationships would become stagnant. This is not to say that sharing karma with a partner is negative. You can share positive karma with a person: you may be fated to meet and start a family again, as you did in a former lifetime. Recognizing the presence of karma between you and your love interest will lead you to work through it and improve your relationship.

You don't have to know the provenance of your karma, but it is helpful to know where and how the issues first started. Often, the work of resolving karma begins with identifying your own patterns and observing how they play out. After that, it takes vigilance to remain observant and make new decisions each time a similar situation comes up and an opportunity for changing habits presents itself. It's especially difficult with the old issues that go back several lifetimes. Mastering karma is not easy, but it absolutely can and must be done. As we'll see shortly, karmic relationships are generally intense, but they are only one of the seven types of relationships that exist.

THE SEVEN TYPES OF LOVE RELATIONSHIPS

Relationships become confusing when our emotions blind us to their true purpose. Deep attachment can force you to stay in a relationship that was meant to end a long time ago, or pride can make you leave a person who's actually your soulmate. At some point in your relationship, you will find yourself asking, "Why is this person in my life? What kind of relationship is this?"

In response to these questions, you could be in any of seven types of love relationships. Each kind of relationship serves a unique purpose to your evolution. You could sustain one or two types of relationship throughout your life or move through the full range of seven. This, again, depends on the interaction between your fate and free will. The relationships you draw in are representative of the amount of inner work you've performed, the lessons your soul agreed to learn, your numerology, and the timing of your life. The following telltale signs of each relationship type will reveal where your love really stands:

TRANSITORY

Most likely to happen in personal years 3, 5, and 9
Most likely to develop between life paths 3 and 7, and 1 and 8

A transitory relationship acts as a bridge between two phases of evolution, enacting change or easing transitions. For example, such a relationship can help a girl become a woman by teaching her first lessons in love, or it may aid a person coping with separation, loss, or divorce until he or she heals and feels ready to embark on new, long-term love.

Transitory relationships are marked by desire, physical chemistry, excitement, and adventure, but they lack commitment and authentic love. Instead, they mostly involve a love of the five senses. Such relationships often commence when a person is feeling vulnerable or right after a serious relationship has ended. The partners in this kind of relationship generally don't become too attached and can let go of each other without much trouble. No serious sacrifices or advancements are being made in a transitory relationship.

This type of relationship is almost always temporary but serves a greater purpose in gently pushing someone from one chapter of life to the next. Once the person evolves, however, the relationship typically fizzles out and is left behind. If you find yourself in a transient relationship, know that it is necessary but only for the time being. Unless genuine emotions arise, your relationship will conclude in the right moment. Don't expect devotion and undying loyalty or you may quickly become discouraged. Simply allow it to run its predestined course. Try not to stress or overthink things; just have fun! This is your time to enjoy yourself and the new person in your life until a better opportunity is placed in your path.

TOXIC

Most likely to happen in personal years 5, 7, and 9
Most likely to develop between life paths 5 and 6, and 7 and 8

A toxic relationship is the most problematic of the seven and the one with the lowest vibrational energy. It is like trying to mix water and oil; you can stir them as much as you'd like, but the two substances will never blend. You might ask why anyone would stay in a relationship that's plagued by constant bickering and never-ending arguments, but you'd be surprised to learn what habit makes of us. Toxic relationships occur when two primary numbers who are simply not meant to be together try to defy all odds. Moreover, on top of the partners being utterly incompatible, the chief reason their relationship turns sour is because they refuse to do their work. By being careless, negligent, and inconsistent, any two people can turn a relationship toxic.

Neither partner in this type of relationship feels good or at peace. Even if the relationship is more toxic for one person than the other, both partners will feel a nagging sense of unease. Toxic relationships are identified by disputes over every little thing. The partners will turn defensive if not downright hostile toward each other, one constantly misinterpreting what the other says and does. One partner could be putting away the dishes and the other will chide him for putting them in the wrong cabinet. There could also be bigger issues at play, such as cheating, manipulation, withholding, or abuse. It is both small and large differences that characterize a toxic relationship; it is never just one matter. Ironically, at the end of the day the partners will return to each other, sometimes like nothing happened. This is because they've gotten used to bonding over their pernicious relationship. Because no work is being done to resolve the plethora of problems, the next day will deliver the same disasters.

This relationship will eventually end, most likely because each partner will have reached his or her limit. Escape from such a relationship is the best thing that could happen for both partners, because it frees them to seek more-normal and more-compatible bonds.

STAGNANT

Most likely to happen in personal years 3, 5, and 8
Most likely to develop between life paths 1 and 5, and 5 and 7

A stagnant relationship can start off great and steadily expand until it reaches a plateau it can't get past. This is the main defining feature of this type of relationship: hitting a brick wall that makes everything stop in its tracks. It's not necessarily that the partners did anything wrong or that they're not performing the right work, like in a toxic relationship, but that the relationship has reached its spiritual capacity. At that point, it cannot get any further. Think about what happens to a body of water that doesn't flow, such as a pond: it becomes dirty and infested with bacteria. A relationship, too, needs to stream forward with momentum and clarity.

Stagnant relationships are prevalent. I am frequently visited by clients who state that their relationship was chugging along smoothly until it hit a bump in the road that caused it to come to a grinding halt. One client recently reported that she had been dating a great guy with whom she got along well, but that several circumstances prevented them from moving in together: either he had to move from his apartment or his daughter from a previous marriage needed a place to stay, preventing my client from moving in. The relationship was never able to move past this hitch and died out. Another client stated that she had met a wonderful man online who lived oversees. The two chatted daily and felt a mutual growing affinity for one another, but seeing each other was next to impossible: the pandemic hit, and after a year of talking over a screen without the possibility of meeting, the couple decided to date people they could actually see face to face. These are just two of many examples of how a relationship can become stagnant.

If the obstacle truly can't be surmounted, then the relationship will come to a close. The timing of when it ends depends on how long either partner wants to hold on to the other, despite not being able to make steps in the right direction. If you find yourself in a stagnant relationship, this is something you'll have to evaluate for yourself: How long can you stand by without making progress? Even if it drags on for a while, a stagnant relationship will dissipate sooner or later.

COMPROMISE

Most likely to happen in personal years 2, 7, and 9
Most likely to develop between life paths 1 and 4, and 4 and 9

A compromise relationship is the most common of the seven types. It occurs when two people form a union based on an arrangement of comfort, such as financial stability or social standing. Many relationships that are meant to end continue because both partners have become so used to each other that they find it difficult to part ways. In short, they settle for one other. They may share a house and have children, which makes them feel obliged to stay together despite the fact that they don't feel fulfilled or fully in love. Relationships based on compromise keep us stuck in a comfort zone. It is crucial to your well-being to evaluate whether you're truly satisfied with your partner, or merely comfortable.

Being in a compromise relationship can become stultifying and downright boring; most result in one or both partners straying outside the relationship for romance, excitement, and love. In the end, most also result in divorce or separation, simply because the perks of comfort can't compare to a genuine connection. In my practice, I often hear my patients declare that their spouse is a great parent to their children and provider for their family, but that they know deep down their relationship is a compromise. They can feel the truth in their hearts but dismiss their intuition. The defining quality of compromise relationships is that one or both partners feel complacent, but not satisfied.

This type of relationship can be complementary, but more in terms of advancing in the physical world: generating income, buying properties, raising the kids, and so on. Each partner follows specific roles and contributes to the success of the couple's mutual goals. In terms of a relationship that's based on arrangement, it becomes the free will of each partner whether to remain together or separate. I've seen compromise relationships that have lasted a lifetime because neither partner wanted to let go of the other, and that's perfectly fine.

If you find yourself in a compromise relationship, know that the decision to stay or go is your own. If you crave a love that will nourish you deeply and wholly, you owe it to yourself to seek your soulmate (yes, you have one!). No matter how comfortable you are or what material gains you've made, it is your birthright to give and receive unconditional love.

COMPLEMENTARY

Most likely to happen in personal years 2, 3, and 6
Most likely to develop between life paths 2 and 3, and 4 and 6

A complementary relationship is stronger than a compromise relationship but a step down from a soulmate bond. Complementary relationships are harmonious and uplifting in nature, with each partner balancing the other physically, emotionally, and mentally. They can still compromise in the sense of coming together for mutual interests such as finances, but there is a special spark in this type of relationship that's not present in a compromise one. Relationships that are complementary are usually for the long term or lifelong; they generally remain consistent and don't diminish with time like transitory, toxic, or stagnant relationships do.

One caveat to those who believe they're in this kind of relationship: you will still experience a fair share of problems. Because there is no smooth sailing in relationships, the partners in a complementary relationship can still fight over little things, disagree on fundamental matters, and split up if they're not mindful. Unlike karmic relationships, which are dictated by an action that has to take place, there is plenty of room for free will in complementary relationships. This means that the partners should regard their relationship as a blank canvas: although you complement each other, the relationship will be what you make of it. Water it, and it will bloom. Neglect it, and it will wither away. Even though it will take a lot to destroy this bond, its integrity can still be broken.

The partners in this relationship can make truly beautiful things happen if they're aware of each other: they can travel the world, raise a happy family, and make lasting memories, among many other things. They can even run a successful business together because they are so compatible. The difference between this and a soulmate relationship is that the partners don't fit each other like two pieces of a puzzle. Even so, they will feel a substantial pull toward one another. Complementary relationships remind us that our choices can be just as powerful as the hand of destiny in shaping the course of a relationship.

KARMIC

Most likely to happen in personal years 1, 4, and 8
Most likely to develop between life paths 4 and 8, and 8 and 8

A karmic relationship is like a stage play: it involves some sort of plot that must unfold within the relationship, such as the breaking of behavioral patterns or cycles of events. This type of relationship denotes past lives shared by two partners; hence a strong feeling of familiarity or "knowing" this person from somewhere. Two souls that have passed through certain experiences together will find each other again to close what was left open.

A karmic relationship is almost always described as intense: when it's good, it's great, and when it's bad, it's awful! But there's instant magnetism from the beginning; the person is simply irresistible to you. This relationship may be prone to disagreements as the two souls try to find solutions to old problems. They may also feel a deep-seated desire to be dutiful or sacrificial for one another, sensing the need to cooperate to reach higher ground. Regardless, those in karmic relationships are guaranteed to learn a lot of necessary lessons, both as a couple and as individuals.

After the karma is settled, however, the relationship may come to an end because its role has been rendered. Sometimes karmic partners can also be soulmates. If they are, the relationship will endure beyond the completion of the karma. Karmic relationships are enriching, progressive, and enlightening, whether temporary or for the long term. If you find yourself in a karmic relationship, you have attracted a soul you knew before. Try to pinpoint the reason why this person is in your life once more: What is it that you must resolve, enact, or change in yourself, in each other, or with each other? For example, maybe your partner hurt you in a past life, and now he or she must make it up to you by helping you in other ways. Or, maybe you had children with this person in a previous lifetime and you've reunited to start a family again. Karmic relationships are powerful and passionate and can be tremendously positive once you grasp the transcendent nature of karma.

SOULMATE

Can happen in any personal year, but most likely to happen in personal years 1 and 6
Most likely to develop between life paths 1 and 9, and 2 and 6

A soulmate relationship is a one-of-a-kind bond reaching deeper than physical or emotional levels. Soulmate relationships are far and few, but when they do occur, they often last the test of time. This kind of relationship is marked by a profound connection between two people, one that may even be difficult to convey. Soulmates just get each other: they can finish each other's sentences, are best friends as well as lovers, and share an "us against the world" mentality.

When two soulmates have found each other, the feeling is likened to two pieces of a puzzle that fit perfectly. Soulmates can't wait to come home to each other after a long day, and they may even be linked telepathically, one partner sensing what the other feels, needs, and fears at all times. They never grow tired of each other and can both work and play together because of how well they complement each other; one elevates the other in thought, potential, and ability. The relationship is spared petty arguments and is bursting with compromise and compassion. This is not to say that soulmates won't stumble into problems along the course of their relationship, but that they'll be able to resolve their issues more easily than couples who aren't bound by soulful ties. Very few things in this world can break up two soulmates, because their connection is otherworldly. Soulmates can also have mutual karma to work on, but unlike in a karmic relationship, they won't sever ties once their past-life business is finished.

If you find yourself in a soulmate relationship, congratulations! This is the purest, highest, and most unconditional type of relationship that exists. Be thankful for your union, because many people wish they could meet their heart's other half. Be as involved in your relationship as possible and dismiss insignificant problems from the outside world. Together, you are a sublime force. Treasure your partner and take joy in every moment by his or her side, knowing that your souls have reunited at last.

It can be difficult to disentangle our emotional knots and understand the core function of a relationship. Detaching ourselves from our feelings just enough to assess the authenticity of our relationship can make a world of a difference in the quality of love we give and gain. Reflect on which of these relationships you've passed through as we explore the nine numerological archetypes in the following chapters.

Refer to the appendix at the back of this book for a quick reference to the seven types of love relationships.

CHAPTER FOUR

LIFE PATH 1: THE INDEPENDENT

I hold my own mind and
think apart from other men.

—Agamemnon, from
Aeschylus's *Agamemnon*

THE INDEPENDENT "HOLDS HIS OWN MIND" because he is firm in his decisions and sound in his logic. This life path stands on his own feet, and it will take a strong storm to knock him down. Seldom does the Independent feel confused and seek guidance from others. If he does, it's from someone he trusts and deems as grounded as him, like a good friend or parent figure. This is not a number likely to be racked with feelings of hopelessness or desperation. He reasons through strife and regains control fairly quickly. The Independent thinks apart from others because he reveres his mental competence and uses it to fortify his sense of identity.

Number 1 venerates his freedom and therefore might be reluctant to enter a relationship in which he'll have to "share" his life with a partner. He is defined by a need to be on his own that holds true not only in his love relationship but in his career: the Independent performs well in positions that allow him to work for and by himself, being well organized, disciplined, and focused on personal progress. Number 1 doesn't look at what others are doing; he proudly carves his own path through life. It's likely that his sense of autonomy was evident from early on: even as a child, the Independent might have taken his toys and gone to play on his own.

Apart from being influenced by his life path, the Independent's sense of self-rule is psychologically linked to notions of success and happiness that were likely imparted on him during childhood. My mother was a 1 and as independent as can be. But her demeanor wasn't owed only to her primary number. Her own mother passed away shortly after she was born, and she was raised by her father and brothers, learning how to be strong and tough from them. She also lived through the Second World War; there were days during which the family had nothing to eat, and when Soviet soldiers invaded Romania, my mother and her siblings had to hide for weeks in a tiny room built behind a wall. She learned that she had to be self-sufficient if she wanted to survive. When she got married and started a family, these instincts remained with her. Circumstances, along with the predilections of her life path, molded my mother into a true Independent archetype.

Unlike the Free Spirit, who experiences commitment problems on a broader spectrum, the Independent has issues pledging himself to a love relationship. Although he has good intentions, his words get stuck in his throat when he's trying to comfort someone. As a result, he doesn't necessarily come across as romantic or emotional. The Independent may not always feel as deeply as others do; they have a psychological gap at the level of bonding with another human being. This may be caused by a fear of losing themselves to a partner. Thus, the Independent subconsciously retains a portion of himself for himself only, which doesn't allow him to become fully dedicated to another person. This life path sometimes erects boundaries that his partner can't cross, always keeping a certain distance from his significant other. From not letting his partner into his personal space to subconsciously sabotaging potential relationships, the Independent builds emotional walls around himself. The moment a partner starts chipping away at these walls and breaches his boundaries, the Independent's flight response kicks in and he recalls how much he cherishes his independence.

The Independent associates strong emotional attachment with commitment he believes is beyond his capacity. This personality type controls his feelings well, and he doesn't expose his weaknesses in any sense of the word. Of the archetypes, Independents are closest to being masters over their emotions. At first, the Independent comes across as engaging, approachable, and sociable. But after some time, he can turn cold, tough, stubborn, and inaccessible. This is his way of letting his partner know that there's a limit to how close she can get.

The Independent values his own abilities more than he values partnership—what he can do for himself over what others can do for him. He's so concerned with meeting his own needs that he can't see someone else fulfilling them. He is needy, as are most people, but he either believes a partner can't meet his needs or that he'll be stripped of his identity if she does. The Independent feels that he's worked hard to preserve his lifestyle and that commitment comes at a serious price. He lives well on his own and has no problem running a household by himself, cooking for himself, and making his own appointments. To the Independent, the freedom of coming and going as he pleases is priceless. He does, however, realize that he *should* be in a relationship. At times he might even think there's something wrong with him for not being tied down by now.

What often ends up being the case with the Independent is that he starts to like a person—even a lot—but then some small thing she does turns him off completely. He then remembers how much he likes being on his own and reverts to old habits. Some might interpret the Independent's conduct as outright rejection, which is not the case. They then push harder and come on more aggressively to get his attention. This is not the right mentality or approach to have with this archetype, not to mention that it's utterly ineffective. The Independent likes to chase, not be chased. Realistic expectations and notions of time are required with this type of person. The person interested in an Independent will have to take baby steps toward commitment. Coming on too strongly will make him run away at the speed of light, right back into his man cave. Some people in this category can conquer their commitment barriers fully, and some only partially. Then there are Independents who remain autonomous for as long as they live, but they've found partners who are able to tolerate them as they are. It's important not to draw any conclusions about your own Independent love interest until you can measure some progress.

The Independent can be pretty introverted in his thoughts and ambitions, choosing not to share what he thinks or wants all the time. But what distinguishes him from an actual Introvert is that he has no problem being the center of attention. He isn't affected by crowds, noise, or parties like a true Introvert; he really enjoys mingling and networking like an Extrovert. The Independent lives within the paradox of being immensely confident in himself yet highly insecure about sharing his life with another person. On the outside, he comes across as charismatic and ready to win over a partner. But on the inside, he feels he can't cope with the demands of a relationship or the needs of another human being. The way he presents himself is inconsistent with the way he thinks, a classic case of cognitive dissonance between wanting a relationship yet blocking potential relationships from taking place. This does not mean the Independent is lonely; he usually has strong ties with family, friends, and coworkers and simply feels more comfortable without a significant other in tow.

The Independent has toyed with the idea of getting into a real relationship in his mind, but the murky waters of commitment pose too great a threat to his liberty. He may even have attempted to get into serious relationships in the past, often unsuccessfully, so he regresses to playing it safe and being on his own. But in his heart, the Independent both realizes he can't stay single forever and doesn't want to be without a partner to call his own. He'd like to be in a relationship, but with a person who's easygoing and highly independent herself. The Independent *can* commit, especially if he's found a partner who "gets" him. This type of person is able to offer commitment if there is understanding and diligence from his partner. If you believe that your Independent is worth the effort, you can take the right actions to get him to become slowly but steadily attached to you.

The Independent needs a partner who's able to give him space. He does not want to hear his partner beg or lay out the obvious logic of why they should spend more time together. He wants his partner to keep busy tending to her own needs. The more she is able do that, the more he comes toward her on his own. His partner shouldn't try to barge into the Independent's life and start doing his laundry or making him breakfast. She might consider these nice gestures, but he'll consider them an invasion of privacy because he's used to doing things for himself a certain way. Communication is key with the Independent; asking him what he wants or needs from you will avoid misunderstandings. Allow the Independent to take the initiative and strike up conversation. With time and patience, the Independent will become steadily more devoted to the partner who lets him retain his identity while offering companionship.

COMPATIBILITY FOR THE INDEPENDENT

The Independent and the Independent (1 and 1)—likely to be in a complementary relationship: Two life path 1s can get along smoothly. If they choose to work together, they can successfully run a business successfully and expand it because each Independent will seriously set sight on his goals. The catch is keeping enough space between them; the moment they become too enmeshed in each other's affairs, they'll end up suffocating each other and quickly get fed up with the relationship. Competition is not a good idea between two of these numbers. If they can stick to their original agreement, they can make it happen. Otherwise, 1s can get snarky and downright rude with each other, especially if they feel their personal space is being invaded. The key is to keep up a positive attitude in this relationship and not let ego control the dynamic. Each

Independent is a powerful person with a strong identity, so it's imperative for the partners to lift each other up and focus on their shared strengths instead of their individual weaknesses; they should remind each other often why they're in a relationship instead of single, as they're used to being. As much as they might like to be on their own and make their own rules, 1s will multiply the potential within each other and recognize that they're a force to be reckoned with if they act as one.

The Independent and the Introvert (1 and 2)—likely to be in a karmic relationship: An Independent and an Introvert have potential because the Introvert can encourage the Independent to bear his softer, more playful side. Once they're intimate, the Introvert can convince the Independent to curb some of his tenacious tendencies and yield to a relationship without fear of losing his identity to another person. But if an Introvert feels he can't trust his Independent partner, he won't exert effort and may give up on the relationship. Because the Introvert treasures his personal space, he will turn their house into a cozy home. This will make the Independent want to come home after being out all day, whether he was working, at the gym, or hanging out with friends. If the 1 gets too carried away with having liberty and ignores the 2, the Introvert will take it the wrong way. He may snap back into his shell (a classic Introvert move) or try to get some answers out of the Independent, the latter of which will make a 1 life path feel asphyxiated. The Introvert will constantly try to get to know the Independent on a deeper level, to figure out what makes him tick, actions the Independent won't necessarily appreciate. If the Introvert respects the Independent's need for freedom and the Independent inspires a sense of trust in the Introvert, this relationship can move along nicely.

The Independent and the Extrovert (1 and 3)—likely to be in a transitory relationship: Independents and Extroverts are somewhat similar in nature: they're both social, charming, and outgoing. Their differences start when they're too critical of each other, since neither partner handles criticism well, even if it comes under a constructive guise. The Extrovert can easily become anxious, and the Independent may seek satisfaction elsewhere. This can be avoided if each partner is careful with his words by not being too blunt or unfiltered with the other. The 1 loves a good challenge, and the 3 likes to be chased. The Extrovert will give his partner attention by paying lots of compliments to the Independent, which the 1 will enjoy because he wants to be reassured that he's doing things well. Because he's goal oriented, the Independent can help the Extrovert focus on his accomplishments. These two numbers will be brimming with excitement when they speak to each other, and can enjoy a stimulating physical relationship. They must remember to look beyond superficial matters and delve beneath the surface, since they both have a tendency to ignore their inner selves. Because their personalities are so alike, these two life paths can enjoy a great relationship so long as their egos are moderated.

The Independent and the Realist (1 and 4)—likely to be in a compromise relationship: This combination can be a bit tricky, particularly because neither the Independent nor the Realist has ample patience for the other—they are notoriously headstrong. The Realist has patience for his assignments but not always for those around him, and the Independent has patience to implement his every whim. The 1 is quick to execute his ideas and follow through on his plans, but the 4 believes that planning is sometimes more important than doing. The Realist needs to be in control of all circumstances, including his relationships, but the last thing the Independent wants is to be controlled. This can lead to frequent clashes of energy between these two numbers. The Realist also wants a partner who will tend to his needs, but the Independent simply isn't willing to dedicate so much time and effort to another person. The dynamic of this relationship is more like an employer and employee: one gives careful instructions and the other puts them into action. What helps is that they're both highly pragmatic. As lovers, however, these life paths have numerous challenges to overcome because of their divergent personalities.

The Independent and the Free Spirit (1 and 5)—likely to be in a stagnant relationship: If ever there was a couple that values freedom, the Independent and Free Spirit is it. Both the 1 and 5 want time apart from each other; they need space to make it work. These are not exactly needy numbers desperate to curl into each other's arms every night; they're fine not seeing each other for a week (or two) and simply checking in once a day. The Independent wants to focus on his ambitions, and the Free Spirit wants to travel and go on adventures. Each will take comfort in the fact that, when all is said and done, there's someone there for him. This kind of relationship, unfortunately, can lead to detachment and easy breakups. They have to be careful not to become too detached from one another, since each archetype can easily become absorbed in his own world; I've seen 1s and 5s fizzle out, not because of underlying problems within the relationship, but because both partners simply lived separate lives. These numbers can have trouble settling down, and after years of dating, their families might start to ask, "When are you getting married? Are you ever going to have children?" Neither will know how to answer such questions, or if there is a right answer at all. When the Independent and Free Spirit do reunite after a break, their enthusiasm will be palpable and their romance will be at its peak. If each partner can live with the other while living apart, this relationship is sustainable.

The Independent and the Hopeless Romantic (1 and 6)—likely to be in a toxic relationship: The problem with this couple isn't that they aren't compatible; it's that one partner will try to do too much for the other. Because the Hopeless Romantic is naturally generous and nurturing, he will try to shower the Independent with attention, which the Independent won't want to accept. Coming on too strongly is a prime way to scare off an Independent, but the Hopeless Romantic won't be deterred one bit; he'll simply push harder. This game of tug-of-war won't lead to a successful relationship. The 1 and 6 partners must learn how to compromise: the Hopeless Romantic will have to grant the Independent his personal space when he needs it, and the Independent will have to allow the Hopeless Romantic to care for him to a certain degree. Both the Hopeless Romantic and Independent will try to do things their way because it is in their characters to get things done, often on their own. These numbers fail to realize that in a relationship, cooperation is key to success. For this pair to work, each partner will have to perform his duties without overstepping the boundaries of the other, and to praise his significant other for his excellent work.

The Independent and the Spiritual Seeker (1 and 7)—likely to be in a stagnant relationship: Figuratively speaking, the partners in this relationship live on separate realms and view life from unrelated angles. The Independent is an animated, action-packed go-getter, while the Spiritual Seeker is a great philosopher of otherworldly matters. The Spiritual Seeker will analyze every aspect of the Independent's strengths and weaknesses, which will greatly annoy the Independent since his identity is tantamount to his existence. Simply put, the 1 does not want the 7 telling him what's wrong with him, especially from some mystical standpoint. When things turn sour, both partners can turn their backs on the other for a while: the Independent will think he's better off on his own, and the Spiritual Seeker will simply leave things up to fate. With this mentality, hell will freeze over before one reaches out to the other. This can result in lack of effort to maintain a serious relationship in time. These two individuals may have conflicting outlooks on life, but if each comes to appreciate and even learn from the other's way of thinking, they can create a beautiful balance between practicality and spirituality.

The Independent and the Workaholic (1 and 8)—likely to be in a transitory relationship: Discipline is the general vibration of this relationship. The Independent and Workaholic are well oriented in the real world and have their heads tightly fastened onto their shoulders. The diligence of each partner is impressive: the Independent is ever striving to improve himself, while the Workaholic is nearly obsessed with making material progress. They make an agreeable couple who respect each other's private needs and personal ambitions, but heaven forbid that they start criticizing each other: harsh words can result in all-out war. The 8 sees himself as the boss of the relationship and, like an employer scolding his employee, will point out the 1's most-painful failings. The Independent will not take lightly this direct sting to his identity. It may cause him to rethink the whole relationship and retreat into solitude once more. After that happens, each partner will start tending to his own goals, and their connection will diminish. They'll have to let each other win once in a while, with the Workaholic watching what he says so as not to bruise the Independent's ego. If these numbers want to last, they'll have to speak and act softly with each other.

The Independent and the Well-Rounded One (1 and 9)—likely to be in a soulmate relationship: This combination makes for a compelling couple that symbolizes two opposing sides of the personality spectrum. The Independent is ego driven, while the Well-Rounded One is propelled by altruism. The Independent dreams about advancing his own aspirations, while the Well-Rounded One dreams of contributing to the greater good. The Independent lives in the moment, while the Well-Rounded One thinks well into the future. Although their ambitions span in different directions, they have significant lessons to learn from each other: the Independent can learn how to focus on what really matters in life, while the Well-Rounded One can learn how to focus on what he wants to achieve for himself. Their common thread is that both partners seek solutions: they are motivated individuals determined to find a way forward, whether it's running a multimillion-dollar business or ending world hunger. Both the 1 and 9 thrive on solutions; they waste no time in resolving matters, and this applies to their relationship too. This, if nothing else, is enough to keep them together.

CHAPTER FIVE

LIFE PATH 2: THE INTROVERT

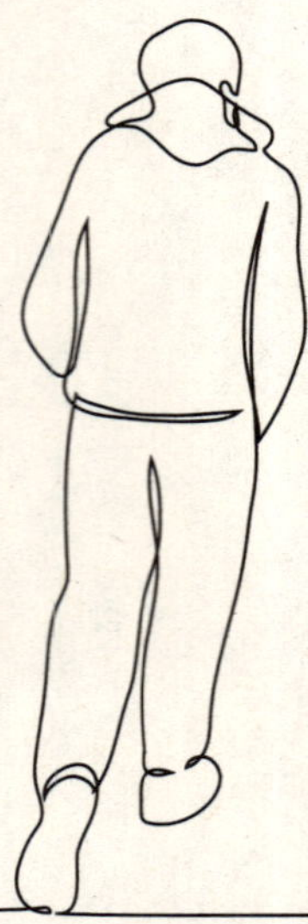

For this feeling of wonder shows that you are a philosopher, since wonder is the only beginning of philosophy.

—Plato

THE INTROVERT IS A PHILOSOPHER; HIS MIND IS HIS PLAYGROUND. In it, he conceives potential ideas and probable solutions with ease. The Introvert's mind houses a microcosm of creative wonder. His mental experiences may feel more real to him than external ones. He places emphasis on the inside before his outside, recognizing the value of having more than good looks or charm. He may appear nondescript, but he has fashioned a colorful inner world: though they express few of their ideas and opinions, Introverts have a million things going on in their minds.

Introverts and Extroverts are two major personality types in psychology. Extroverts are more prominent in our world, and it's easier to spot an Extrovert: sociable, bold, and comfortable in the spotlight. Other archetypes, such as the Independent and Workaholic, are also noticeably extroverted. But how do you recognize an Introvert? Some people think Introverts are the wallflowers at a party, and they're partly right. The giveaway, however, won't be that he's shy or socially awkward or prefers staying in to going out (though he probably will). Many Introverts are excellent at camouflaging themselves as Extroverts! The Introvert's markers are mental: the way he processes reality divulges his true nature, melding facts and imagination to illustrate the world around him. An Introvert's rich personality will reveal itself in his close connections.

This archetype is silently compelling and has an allure that's unique to him: an innate sense of mystery that surrounds him, a quiet sort of language that speaks volumes. He doesn't gain attention through comedic exhibitions or a larger-than-life personality, but through his meek magnetism. The Introvert is the kind of person browsing through some old volume in a bookstore or typing on his laptop in the corner of a coffee shop. But when he looks up and fixes you with a furtive gaze, you instantly want to find out much, much more.

The Introvert is understated but undoubtedly powerful: what you see by looking at him is only the tip of the iceberg. And what you soon discover is that the Introvert's biggest problem is his lack of communication. This can be misinterpreted by his partner as something done on purpose, but in truth, this life path simply prefers keeping things to himself. A person can turn inward after a distressing ordeal, but on the whole, introversion is typically the result of nature, not nurture. The Introvert's gentle disposition developed during his childhood, and his reservations are not based on former experiences. They are ingrained into his personality.

Number 2 contends with his hesitation to trust and his inability to express what he feels. There exists a discrepancy between what's kept on the inside and what's shown on the outside, but not in a harmful way. While he doesn't normally self-destruct, the Introvert does need to uncage some of his inner being and introduce it to the outer world. He needs to realize that it's okay to share: his abundant emotions, his vast knowledge, and his fascinating theories about the world. The Introvert needs to know that he can have a tremendous impact on others if he simply opens up. One of the reasons he might be reluctant to do so is because the Introvert is very stable within himself. He can answer his own questions, form his own opinions, and follow his stellar intuition without fail. Rarely does the Introvert turn to others for assistance;

he believes that within himself is all the help he needs. People vent to the Introvert and regurgitate their life stories (often without the Introvert's invitation), but he seldom shares his own experiences. His art is listening, not talking.

Because the Introvert already has everything he needs inside, he'll let in only those people who can contribute to his stability. He's like a steel fortress that very few can access; to enter, you must show that you come bearing good intentions. The Introvert thinks it's better to keep things to himself, and this is not necessarily because he doesn't trust but because he thinks his partner might not grasp his special way of thinking.

Introverts take a longer time thinking things over and making relevant decisions than their extroverted counterparts. They feel the need to hold a mental exchange before they can come up with a choice, weighing every side to the story. This makes them feel more secure in their decisions. Because Introverts are emotionally intelligent, they also take into consideration the way they feel. If you ask an Introvert for advice on making a decision, he'll probably ask you two things: how you feel about it and what happened the last time you made that decision. If the Free Spirit is impulsive, the Introvert is compulsive; when an unpleasant thought enters his mind, he will study it a thousand times from every angle until he can either reconcile it or make sense of it. Because of this, Introverts can turn obsessive. If you give the Introvert a task, expect that it might take him a bit longer than most people to complete but that he will execute it without flaw.

Because Extroverts are the prevalent archetype, many people aren't sure how to interpret the Introvert. It can be difficult to discern whether the Introvert is really into someone or not, since he doesn't always divulge his feelings. Since society has taught us that men should be in charge, some women deem the Introvert's timidity as a deal-breaker. Unless his partner is also an Introvert, this primary number can be a challenge to decode. Most partners will become frustrated with the Introvert's caution and reticence.

Too many external stimuli at once are unpleasant to the Introvert, since his senses are easily overloaded. The Introvert is perfectly content with curling up with a good book instead of attending an over-the-top party. He prefers predictability over surprises. When he does go out for fun, the Introvert gets tired quickly. He can feel a little anxious, overanalyzing what other people think of him or even imagining that they're saying bad things. This life path is likely to feel exhausted after a long day or night of interactions, because he absorbs even the most-minute details in his surroundings, noticing things that other people easily miss. He likes to plan how many hours he'll spend out and about so that he doesn't become overwhelmed. It's important to encourage the Introvert to have a healthy social life so that he doesn't shrink too far into a solitary world.

After they open up, 2s make loyal partners. Their sense of security is fundamental to them, so they will cling to the person they associate with safety. The Introvert can gift his partner with intimacy, both emotional and physical. Once he's committed, the Introvert's instinctive sense of secrecy will guarantee that his relationship remains private and free of external influences. In the Introvert's eyes, it will be he and his other half above all. The Introvert can become deeply attached if his partner succeeds in breaking through his emotional and mental boundaries. Becoming comfortable with a person and feeling confident enough to share thoughts and ideas is critical to the Introvert. Knowing that his partner won't hurt him will increase the Introvert's vulnerability. His significant other must be careful not to disappoint the Introvert by giving away his secrets or falling short on promises. He's a sensitive person, and this can set the relationship back several giant steps. Since this is a highly imaginative archetype, the Introvert must have his creativity stimulated at all times. If his partner ever so gently unravels his emotional defenses, she can conciliate the Introvert.

The Introvert's commitment problems stem from his doubts and inaccessibility. He needs time to get comfortable, after which he'll become less reserved and confess his views of the world and what has happened in his past. But his partner shouldn't take small progress for granted; if his privacy is invaded too quickly, the Introvert will retreat into hiding like a turtle snapping back into its shell. The first thing the Introvert needs to feel from his partner is trustworthiness. The more he feels at ease with another person, the more he will open up. A whole new side of the Introvert will be unveiled once he's warmed up to his partner: a playful personality, brilliant mind, and witty sense of humor. The Introvert becomes extroverted around the people he trusts. Even though he'll still need his personal space, the Introvert will forge a deep mental connection with his better half.

COMPATIBILITY FOR THE INTROVERT

The Introvert and the Independent (2 and 1)—likely to be in a karmic relationship: An Independent and an Introvert have potential because the Introvert can encourage the Independent to bare his softer, more playful side. Once they're intimate, the Introvert can convince the Independent to curb some of his tenacious tendencies and yield to a relationship without fear of losing his identity to another person. But if an Introvert feels he can't trust his Independent partner, he won't exert effort and may give up on the relationship. Because the Introvert treasures his personal space, he will turn their house into a cozy home. This will make the Independent want to come home after being out all day, whether he was working, at the gym, or hanging out with friends. If the 1 gets too carried away with having liberty and ignores the 2, the Introvert will take it the wrong way. He may snap back into his shell (a classic Introvert move) or try to get some answers out of the Independent, the latter of which will make a 1 life path feel asphyxiated. The Introvert will constantly try to get to know the Independent on a deeper level, to figure out what makes him tick, actions the Independent won't necessarily appreciate. If the Introvert respects the Independent's need for freedom and the Independent inspires a sense of trust in the Introvert, this relationship can move along nicely.

The Introvert and the Introvert (2 and 2)—likely to be in a karmic relationship: Two Introverts make a harmonious couple. They will enjoy each other's company, turn their house into a cozy home, and share a closely forged relationship—that is, if they can overcome one hurdle first: bare their true selves to each other. Introverts don't take love lightly. They see letting another person into their vivid inner world as one of the highest forms of vulnerability. Introverts are innately hesitant to trust, and this hesitancy is doubled when two 2s come together. At the same time, they are prone to giving plenty of love if they can simply let their guard down. Even after they've grown close, the 2s will still need to respect each other's personal space. Since members of this life path harbor the majority of their thoughts inside, there will be many carefully guarded secrets in this relationship if a sense of mutual trust hasn't been established. But if each succeeds to lovingly conquer the other, two Introverts can enjoy a fulfilling, honest, and profound relationship. They will shower each other with innovative ideas and useful suggestions on how to improve their individual lives and mutual relationship. Each will be keen to decipher what makes the other tick, but neither partner will mind this, because once an Introvert has opened up, he is fully faithful to his other half.

The Introvert and the Extrovert (2 and 3)—likely to be in a complementary relationship: They say opposites attract, and they certainly do in the case of an Introvert and Extrovert forming a union. The numbers 2 and 3 contrast in the ways they handle attention and communicate with others: the Extrovert loves to be in the spotlight delivering a speech, while the Introvert prefers to be behind the curtain, silently watching his beloved with swelling pride. There is no competition here; the Introvert will gladly take the back seat so long as his talents are being acknowledged by his significant other. Both partners are wildly creative in their own rights: the Introvert could write an excellent screenplay, and the Extrovert could give a rousing performance in the film. As with all other combinations that involve an Introvert, the 3 must first win his partner's trust in order to enjoy a great relationship with the 2. If he feels neglected by or distrustful of his partner—since the Extrovert can have a wandering eye—the Introvert will choose to start keeping his thoughts and emotions to himself, which can become the bane of this relationship. The Extrovert must make an effort in equal measure to peel off his mask and reveal the deeper layers of his personality to his partner.

The Introvert and the Realist (2 and 4)—likely to be in a compromise relationship: The Introvert and Realist make a couple with potential but in need of work; this is a relationship in which sensitivity and sense mingle, where imagination and discipline meet. The 2 can offer the 4 the attention of which he's so needy, but he must first feel comfortable enough to be himself around his partner. This will take some patience on the part of the Realist, but it will be worth it. Both partners in this relationship are calculated and tactful, with the Introvert having the added bonus of superb intuition. He can guide the Realist when he's not seeing the bigger picture or stuck in a conundrum. In turn, the Realist will enjoy providing stability to his partner and meeting his significant other's every need. As down to earth as he is, the Realist will indulge in the Introvert's creativity and dreams for the future; the 2's prolific mind is like a breath of fresh air to the strict and rigid 4. He must take care not to be too inflexible, which can offend the Introvert. Both partners depend on themselves for answers, yet both can teach each other the value of seeking guidance from their other half when in need.

The Introvert and the Free Spirit (2 and 5)—likely to be in a compromise relationship: This relationship requires work. The Introvert will want to stay home and curl up with a good book, which the Free Spirit will find terribly boring. The Free Spirit craves action and adventure, something the Introvert rarely desires. In fact, too much commotion leaves the Introvert emotionally drained. It has the opposite effect on the Free Spirit, recharging his batteries and amplifying his energy. The Free Spirit will take the liberty to plan the couple's copious activities, which the Introvert won't exactly look forward to since he holds sacred the comfort of his home. The Introvert needs deep intellectual stimulation to feel satisfied, but the Free Spirit just wants to explore and experience different things. The 2 will try to share his sentiments with the 5, but the Fee Spirit might not always understand the breadth of his partner's feelings. It is crucial for the Introvert to refrain from pushing the Free Spirit's buttons or infringing upon his liberties, and it's equally important for the Free Spirit to put effort into getting to know the Introvert truly and deeply. If the Free Spirit doesn't inspire trust in the Introvert, their relationship will simply dissolve. These two numbers must share at least some core values if they want to survive as a couple.

The Introvert and the Hopeless Romantic (2 and 6)—likely to be in a soulmate relationship: This is a couple that can last a lifetime. They share many essential elements in common, such as comfort, compassion, and the ideal of family. The Introvert wants a partner he can trust, while the Hopeless Romantic wants to prove his trustworthiness to his partner: they fit like hand and glove. The Hopeless Romantic must remember not to overindulge the Introvert and to allow him time alone so that the 2 can reflect on his emotions and reenergize himself, and the Introvert needs to reassure the Hopeless Romantic that he's doing a great job of making him happy. Together, they can work magic around the house, adding personal touches around every corner. These archetypes don't like surprises; they appreciate predictability above all and seek it in each other. Few things hurt them more than suffering disappointment at the hands of the person they love, so each has learned the importance of not letting his significant other down. The Hopeless Romantic will put the Introvert at the center of his world and do everything in his power to please him. The Introvert will sense his good intentions and welcome the Hopeless Romantic into his imaginative world.

The Introvert and the Spiritual Seeker (2 and 7)—likely to be in a stagnant relationship: Both the Introvert and the Spiritual Seeker have a strong sense of intuition, which will attract them to one another; they will be drawn to each other's silent appeal. From there, it becomes the free will of both partners to make it work, because this relationship won't come without challenges: the Spiritual Seeker can be out of touch with the Introvert, who needs to feel strongly bonded to his partner at all times. The 7 is a step above the 2 in the field of metaphysics, always seeking the higher realities of life. The Introvert is more leveled with this world, enmeshed in his own thoughts and seeking comfort within himself by the way of his emotions. If the Spiritual Seeker is not firm in his faith, the Introvert will feel like his partner is being cynical, which can lead to their breakup. And if the Introvert refuses to open up to the Spiritual Seeker, the 7 won't spend too much time convincing him to do so. The Spiritual Seeker has to be aligned with the Introvert's feelings to keep his partner from feeling lonely in the relationship.

The Introvert and the Workaholic (2 and 8)—Likely to be in a transitory relationship: The Workaholic will take the lead in this relationship because he always needs a partner who follows him. The Introvert won't mind and will gladly allow his partner to go first, so long as the Workaholic recognizes his efforts. The Workaholic can at times be too straightforward with the Introvert and hurt his feelings without meaning to; this is the way of the 8, brutally honest because he believes in constructive criticism. He forgets that his partner is a delicate being and not a paid employee. When the 2 feels distraught, he will recede into his mind and become distant with his partner. If the Workaholic loses the trust he's worked hard to earn from the Introvert, it will prove nearly impossible to regain. To avoid this, the Workaholic must watch his words when addressing the Introvert, especially under tense emotions. He also needs to know when to pause work and applaud the Introvert's unique and detailed way of doing things. The energy between these partners should be kept in balance so that the Introvert doesn't feel beneath the Workaholic in any way.

The Introvert and the Well-Rounded One (2 and 9)—likely to be in a complementary relationship: This is another match that can work beautifully. The Introvert can uplift the Well-Rounded One to become the greatest version of himself, and the Well-Rounded One can inspire the Introvert to hone his immense creative powers. These two partners can embark on a meaningful project together, with the Introvert working out the finer details and the Well-Rounded One getting the message out to the world. Although the Well-Rounded One likes to put on a strong front, the Introvert will pick up on little things that might be bothering his partner, no matter how much the Well-Rounded One insists that he's fine; the 9 needs this sort of subtlety to remind him that people care about him as much as he cares about them. The Well-Rounded One wants to work for the greater good, but he might push himself beyond his limits in trying to do so. When this happens, the Introvert will reassure the Well-Rounded One that he's done more than enough, and prompt him to take a break. The 2 will treasure the 9's sense of integrity and honesty, which will empower the Introvert to reveal his innermost self without fear. This partnership is a good balance between working to improve yourself and working to improve the world.

CHAPTER SIX

LIFE PATH 3: THE EXTROVERT

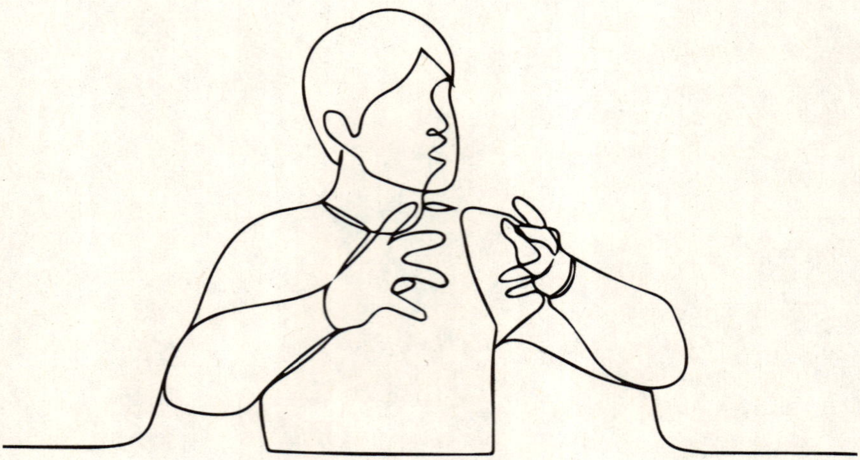

You will never do anything in this world without courage. It is the greatest quality of the mind next to honor.

—Aristotle

Think of the Extrovert as the Great Gatsby: he is charming, communicative, social, attractive, and darn lucky. He can host out-of-this-world parties and sway a crowd with his persuasive air and magnificent presence. Being in the spotlight is associated with discomfort to the Introvert. But to the Extrovert, it's second nature.

Number 3s must externalize their creativity to be happy; when they aren't creating, they're causing drama. Members of this life path are guilty of embellishing the truth when their imagination is in overdrive. They must have a healthful outlet to highlight their creative talents and diffuse them to the world. Extroverts have a knack for networking and transcribing the needs of one person to another.

The Extrovert is an external archetype: much of his energy is concentrated on how he expresses himself to the outside world. He cares about how he looks and comes across to others; he needs to make himself appear attractive in every sense of the word. An Extrovert might take extra time getting ready just to go to the supermarket because he'll be seen by other people, even if they're strangers shopping for their own groceries. Being found riveting and captivating gives this life path a natural high. He is constantly seeking new ways of expression and can weave creativity in magic ways: he makes a fitting artist, musician, thespian, dancer, or performer. In fact, every Extrovert is an actor in his own right. Even if acting isn't his career, he will integrate entertainment into his job. The Extrovert could be a banker—or some other run-of-the-mill profession—but he will use his flair to attract new clients and coax them into opening an account. An Extrovert's mind is sharp and bright but also irascible and impatient.

A 3's natural inclination to perform is bound to extend into his relationship. This can pose a problem, because his partner won't know when he's acting and when he's being himself. At times, the Extrovert may even have trouble making this distinction himself: he can become so engrossed in playing a "character" that he's unable to return to his true self when needed. One disadvantage of being in a relationship with this archetype is that his partner won't always know when he's being himself or when he's taking on a role, when he's telling the truth or when he's lying. His significant other will yearn to know the Extrovert on the inside, but this may prove more difficult than expected. Like an actor, the Extrovert may demonstrate mood swings, teetering on top of the world at one second and then wallowing in misery the next.

In contrast to the Introvert, who reaches the very marrow of his being, the Extrovert's focus is external, so much so that the Extrovert neglects his internal self by choice. He can easily forget his duties to his higher self, like really getting to know himself and delving into the different compartments of his mind. Entertaining a crowd doesn't intimidate him, interestingly enough, but coming face to face with his shadow does. He willfully chooses not to explore the endless depths beneath his exterior, and this comes with a price. The Extrovert can get so caught up in external stimuli that he simply forgets that the world on the inside is much more fascinating than the world on the outside. When we become too dependent on the five senses, we forget that our spirits, not our bodies, house the essence of our being. This is a truth the Extrovert must relearn.

One consequence of this is that the Extrovert can be naive, like a teenager who still believes in Santa. You can imagine that this doesn't play out in his favor when it comes to relationships; the Extrovert can become easily distracted, salivating after partners who steal his attention but have no intention to settle down. Because he doesn't deal well with rejection, this primary number may continue chasing the person who hurts or ignores him. He may also exhibit commitment problems since he hasn't done enough inner work to uphold a serious relationship. If he does find a good partner, the Extrovert might make the mistake of letting his eyes (and hands) wander. He can also be irresponsible with money and finances, thinking he'll "win big" with various types of investments. Even if he loses, this number is convinced that luck will come around again next time. Indeed, Extroverts are like big kids who don't want to grow up; even in their 50s, they'll have an air of playfulness about them.

But luck *is* often on his side, and number 3 bounces back quickly from defeat; he's usually back to his "old self" in a few days. A harrowing ordeal, however, will leave him reeling. This life path won't be sure how to handle pain or heal from the inside out. Because he's a stranger to his inner self, the Extrovert won't know how to effectively process emotions when he's suddenly confronted with them. He might try to ignore them, bury what he feels, or let negative energy linger, lashing out at those around him. He can feel overwhelmed by his own emotions and enter a depressive state if he doesn't effectively mollify his feelings and come to terms with what has transpired.

The Extrovert is intrinsically optimistic, and sooner rather than later he'll start to look on the bright side of things again. Even if he's feeling better, it does not mean he should continue ignoring his inner self. The Extrovert must master the task of digging beneath the surface and reaching his reservoir of substance. Otherwise, he risks being regarded by others as frivolous and one-dimensional. His innate positivity extends into his relationships: the Extrovert seeks solutions to old problems with his partner and looks to improve his dynamic with his better half. He feels best when the relationship is flowing effortlessly, with no pressure or stress from either side. The Extrovert is mostly carefree, so he's turned off by a person who picks fights over little things or incessantly brings up the past. He is thankful for a partner who supports his creative talents. He will adore the other half who believes in him, gives him pep talks, and asks how rehearsal went. In return, the Extrovert will fervently endorse her pursuits too.

If there's one thing the Extrovert dislikes, it's rejection, whether from a lover or friend; he needs to be liked or he'll feel a great sense of unease. He may not recognize this feeling for what it is, but the Extrovert has insecurities too. Within this archetype is a need to be surrounded by company, perhaps too often. His partner may not always get the privacy she needs, since the Extrovert enjoys having friends over (sometimes in the middle of the night, whom he'll probably ask to crash on the couch). This can create a gap for external influences to interfere in the couple's intimacy. His partner might feel the need to "go deeper" into the relationship, but the Extrovert will assure her that he's fine where he is. A 3 isn't the ideal person to expect to sit under a starry sky and deliberate the mysteries of the universe (a Spiritual Seeker would be more appropriate for this activity). Although Extroverts are wildly romantic, there are limits to how much they will reveal about themselves, not only to their other half but to themselves.

A 3's life lesson is to attain mental balance and not veer to emotional extremes that lead to a crash. When he is in a state of harmony, the Extrovert will allow only healthful relationships into his life and become acquainted with his soul. If he has chosen to function at a high frequency, this life path brings joy and comfort to those around him, connecting with them beyond superficial matters. But if he vibrates at a low frequency, he's prone to gossiping about others, bickering with his family members, and spilling his friends' secrets. The Extrovert has a special sense of duality within him; whether he chooses to live on the inside or the outside is up to him, but one or the other will result in a completely different comportment.

COMPATIBILITY FOR THE EXTROVERT

The Extrovert and the Independent (3 and 1)—likely to be in a transitory relationship: Independents and Extroverts are somewhat similar in nature: they're both social, charming, and outgoing. Their differences start when they're too critical of each other, since neither partner handles criticism well, even if it comes under a constructive guise. The Extrovert can easily become anxious, and the Independent may seek satisfaction elsewhere. This can be avoided if each partner is careful with his words by not being too blunt or unfiltered with the other. The 1 loves a good challenge, and the 3 likes to be chased. The Extrovert will give his partner attention by paying lots of compliments to the Independent, which the 1 will enjoy because he wants to be reassured that he's doing things well. Because he's goal oriented, the Independent can help the Extrovert focus on his accomplishments. These two numbers will be brimming with excitement when they speak to each other and can enjoy a stimulating physical relationship. They must remember to look beyond superficial matters and delve beneath the surface, since they both have a tendency to ignore their inner selves. Because their personalities are so alike, these two life paths can enjoy a great relationship so long as their egos are moderated.

The Extrovert and the Introvert (3 and 2)—likely to be in a complementary relationship: They say opposites attract, and they certainly do in the case of an Introvert and Extrovert forming a union. The numbers 2 and 3 contrast in the ways they handle attention and communicate with others: the Extrovert loves to be in the spotlight delivering a speech, while the Introvert prefers to be behind the curtain, silently watching his beloved with swelling pride. There is no competition here; the Introvert will gladly take the back seat so long as his talents are being acknowledged by his significant other. Both partners are wildly creative in their own rights: the Introvert could write an excellent screenplay, and the Extrovert could give a rousing performance in the film. As with all other combinations that involve an Introvert, the 3 must first win his partner's trust in order to enjoy a great relationship with the 2. If he feels neglected by or distrustful of his partner—since the Extrovert can have a wandering eye—the Introvert will choose to start keeping his thoughts and emotions to himself, which can become the bane of this relationship. The Extrovert must make an effort in equal measure to peel off his mask and reveal the deeper layers of his personality to his partner.

The Extrovert and the Extrovert (3 and 3)—likely to be in a compromise relationship: Two Extroverts make a dynamic couple if they're both reverberating at high levels. They see the world as their playground and love to brainstorm, share exciting ideas, and embark on new projects. But if one partner is at his all-time low while the other is at the epitome of success, problems may arise; Extroverts don't do well when they're down on their luck, because they get caught up in their own minds. Both 3s need to ensure they're equally contributory to the relationship and committed to each other, choosing to uplift one another at all times. Because they get distracted easily, they'll have to remind themselves not to yield to temptation, and to remain loyal. They must also break the surface and delve into each other's intimacy. These partners possess competitive tendencies, even with each other! Extroverts want to be the utmost in all they do, not because they're narcissistic but because they're highly ambitious individuals. The cardinal element in this relationship is for each 3 life path to remain within the realm of positivity as much as possible. Then, they can stretch their creative scopes together.

The Extrovert and the Realist (3 and 4)—likely to be in a toxic relationship: The main difference between these partners lies in the ways they approach decision-making. The Realist is pragmatic and tactful, ensuring he has control over all the variables before he proceeds. The Extrovert, on the other hand, likes to throw caution to the wind and dive headlong into choices that aren't always well calculated. If they're planning dinner, the 3 will want to go "wherever there's a good crowd," while the 4 will scour the restaurant's reviews, make reservations, and confirm them twice. Both these archetypes are concerned with their appearance, so an Extrovert and Realist couple can come across as vain if shallow tendencies aren't mitigated. It's necessary for these partners to learn the value of sacrificing for one another and the rewards that come with giving without expecting to receive. All in all, one balances the energy of the other. An Extrovert can show a Realist the beauty of human connections and letting loose once in a while, and a Realist can teach an Extrovert that careful planning ensures success. They make an excellent couple to work on a project: the Realist will set up the logistics and the Extrovert will handle publicity.

The Extrovert and the Free Spirit (3 and 5)—likely to be in a transitory relationship: Spontaneity spells out the union between these partners, who are ready to pack their bags and travel across the world on a whim. Both tend to dive into their decisions, yes, but the Extrovert knows a limit to the risks he takes, whereas the Free Spirit does not. The 5 is not just friendly and sociable—he can be downright reckless, which is something the 3 is not. The Free Spirit's indecisiveness will affect this relationship (as it does all areas of his life), and his inability to commit will turn off the Extrovert, who is perfectly capable of being in a serious relationship in spite of his outgoing personality. The moment the Extrovert becomes judgmental of his partner and gives him a piece of his mind, the Free Spirit might reconsider the relationship, collect his belongings, and leave. The Extrovert will waste no time in finding a replacement, which is not the right approach either. There is a desperate demand for heartfelt communication between these numbers and a need to learn how to navigate through rough waters instead of abandoning ship. On a lighter note, you can be sure that an Extrovert and a Free Spirit will steal the spotlight the moment they waltz into a party together.

The Extrovert and the Hopeless Romantic (3 and 6)—likely to be in a compromise relationship: This relationship abounds with passion . . . of two different kinds: the Extrovert's passion for life and the Hopeless Romantic's passion for his partner. The Hopeless Romantic will embolden the Extrovert in all his endeavors, whether they are wise or foolish. In return, the Extrovert will give the Hopeless Romantic plenty of attention. But when one partner does not feel adequately cared for in this relationship, their discrepancies become pronounced: if the 6 does not feel appreciated, he will push harder for his partner to recognize his efforts. If the 3 feels undervalued (which is unlikely, since the Hopeless Romantic lives to please), he might seek attention elsewhere. If the Extrovert is the one to lose interest, the Hopeless Romantic is unlikely to relinquish him, and the relationship can turn into a chasing game. The relationship doesn't have to reach this point if the partners find new ways of feeding their fervor for one another. The Extrovert will feel excited to return to a comfortable and beautifully decorated home, courtesy of the Hopeless Romantic, every night.

The Extrovert and the Spiritual Seeker (3 and 7)—likely to be in a transitory relationship: These partners can unveil new worlds to each other. The Spiritual Seeker is profound and probing in nature, and the Extrovert is superficial and upbeat. The Spiritual Seeker can inspire his partner to reach within and question his existence, while the Extrovert can teach his partner how to live in the present and enjoy the moment. A conversation between the 3 and 7 might consist of the Extrovert telling the Spiritual Seeker, "This is how it is," to which the Spiritual Seeker will respond, "But what if . . . ?" As long as each respects the other's opinions, theirs can be a long and lasting alliance. It will seriously offend his partner if one starts to think that his way of thinking and doing holds more merit than the other's; neither of these two archetypes likes to be critiqued or have their beliefs questioned. They will express different levels of communication that complement each other: the Extrovert can show the Spiritual Seeker how to release pent-up thoughts without restraint, and the Spiritual Seeker can guide the Extrovert to investigate his feelings without necessarily acting on them.

The Extrovert and the Workaholic (3 and 8)—likely to be in a compromise relationship: An Extrovert and a Workaholic must find a greater reason to stay together, or they will quickly part ways. The 3 will feel neglected by the 8, who pores over his work and tasks night and day. Conversely, the Workaholic will feel frustrated by the Extrovert's lack of foundation and foggy vision for his future. Because his skill is communication, the Extrovert won't hold back when it comes to telling the Workaholic exactly how he feels and what his partner is doing wrong, which won't sit well with the Workaholic. He will retaliate by reminding the Extrovert of everything he's done for him and can even go as far as to deem him ungrateful. Because these life paths utter bitter words under strain, their conversations can turn sour and damage what could otherwise be a promising relationship. To ameliorate such situations, the Workaholic can gently press the Extrovert to dedicate himself to his projects, while the Extrovert can keep busy and let the Workaholic perform his work duties in peace. Both archetypes must learn to hold their tongues at times and express emotions in a less vitriolic way.

The Extrovert and the Well-Rounded One (3 and 9)—likely to be in a complementary relationship: The beauty of this relationship is that the Well-Rounded One can teach the Extrovert how to expand his potential to do good and use his gift of gab for a greater purpose. In turn, the Extrovert will show the Well-Rounded One how to deliver his message to a larger audience and influence more people with his work. The Well-Rounded One's principle of altruism paired with the Extrovert's communicative creativity can mobilize this couple to start a campaign that's bigger than both of them; they can leave a legacy behind if their powers are used to enact positivity in the world. Both partners are social and demonstrative, and they do well when their conversations transcend gossip or trends. In the intimacy of their home, the 9 will push the 3 to analyze himself beneath his facade, while the 3 will defend the 9 through any family drama. Theirs will be a mostly peaceful relationship, but the Well-Rounded One is more likely to be loyal than the Extrovert. The Extrovert should aspire to reach the apex of self-control, as the Well-Rounded One has, for the sake of his own personal evolution.

CHAPTER SEVEN

LIFE PATH 4: THE REALIST

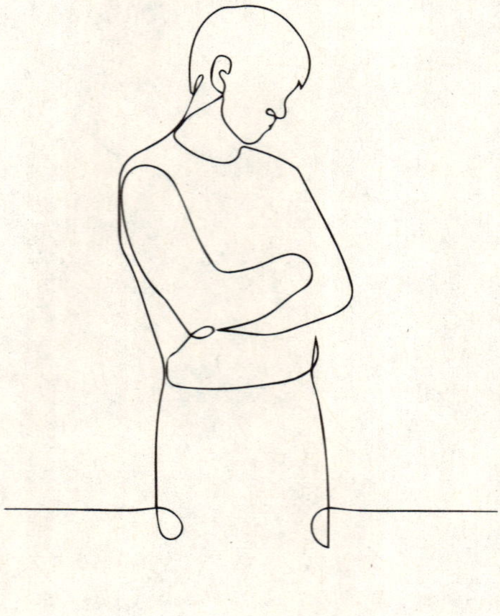

Those who know, do. Those who understand, teach.

—Aristotle

THE REALIST IS AS DOWN TO EARTH AS IT GETS. Unlike the Hopeless Romantic, a notorious daydreamer, or the Spiritual Seeker, a pursuer of esoteric knowledge, number 4 is a rationalist. He recognizes that he is bound by the laws of the physical world, and thus he works with them to his favor. He is orderly, pragmatic, and self-reliant, all qualities that benefit him. Inside his head is a terribly busy but impeccably organized brain. He does things on his own terms and time and is unwilling to change that. The Realist can be stubborn and close minded but has an extraordinary talent for taking things as they are. He accepts all situations—wonderful and awful—with such alacrity that it's unnerving. His saving grace is not only acceptance, but transmutation: the Realist can take any situation and turn it around. Oprah Winfrey was born into poverty in rural Mississippi and was molested during childhood. She even became pregnant at the age of 14 and lost a baby that was born prematurely. Despite this, Oprah transformed a life of setbacks and hardships into success and fame. Such is the power of the Realist to shift encumbrances into advantages.

Security is synonymous with the Realist. This life path needs to feel secure on all levels: in his home, job, relationship, and mind. This makes him a level-headed archetype, with logic lending him control. In seeking peace of mind, however, the Realist may stay in a bad relationship simply because he doesn't want to lose the (sometimes false) sense of security it brings.

If he dwells on the negative side of his personality, the Realist can lose touch with humanity and become desensitized to the needs of others. In contrast to the Well-Rounded One, who is a true altruist, a Realist who operates at a low frequency will be seduced by personal pursuits and neglect the more important things in life.

It's not that the Realist is emotionally inept; he can develop deep and palpable feelings for his love interest. Just because this life path is rational to a fault doesn't mean he can't be loving, dependable, and giving. The issue is that too many of the Realist's feelings concern himself; 4s are not cold hearted, but some are more in touch with themselves than they are with their partners. The ego serves a central role in protecting us from harm, and when we act on our ego, we make decisions that serve us. But when our ego gets carried away, it makes us do things that appear selfish, uncaring, and disrespectful. We start to think *only* about ourselves and little or not at all about others. The Realist's ego can overpower the more empathetic aspects of his personality; he is already proud to begin with. Ironically, this tendency can emerge from an inferiority complex: the Realist is concerned that he might not be as good as, as rich as, as good looking as, or as powerful as others. To alleviate these intimidations, he puts extra effort into proving he's the best. Deep down, the Realist cares what others think—*a lot*.

To the Realist, life is all or nothing. The 4 refuses to carry out an idea until it has been seamlessly developed and can be perfectly executed. No one performs a well-ordered task better than the Realist. Solving a puzzle, creating a meal from scratch, and even building a house all are activities at which the Realist excels. His favorite sort of alchemy is working with his hands and mind to transform ideas into tangible objects. Unlike many people, Realists love long assignments that can be performed step by step and with precision. They will get so absorbed in their craft that they'll forget there's an outside world. In many instances, they'll become experts in what they're creating, outdoing even the person who taught them how to perform the task in the first place. Exercises that reduce activity in the brain, such as writing, meditating, or simply sitting quietly in nature, can keep this number from succumbing to addiction. When life becomes disorderly, the Realist can start to feel anxious. Activities that give the 4 a break from his constantly grinding brain ground him. Slow and steady wins the race, according to this archetype.

Realists can give off mixed signals at first: does this person like me or does he never want to see me again? This life path won't jump to give you a warm hug and kiss on both cheeks; his is a quiet and reserved nature that makes him come across as haughty. The Realist is neither mean nor cold, but he needs time to warm up to new people. After he does, his captivating character emerges. Similarly, if he doesn't like you, he'll make it known with one steely glance. The Realist keeps his thoughts to himself and doesn't appreciate others trying to pry into his mind. Like a Spiritual Seeker, this primary number doesn't need a lot of people in his life to feel fulfilled. Quality over quantity, he will tell you.

Because he's acutely aware, the Realist who vibrates highly sees his defects and wants to correct them. Those who live on the simpler side of this archetype won't admit their faults or try to mollify them; they'll play up their strengths and make them known to the world. The irony is that in wanting to be the best of the best, this life path will try to please his partner in every way. He will make sure that if they split, she remembers him as the best thing that ever happened to her. True to his character, he'll take the lead in his relationship and go out of his way to prove that he's a better partner than any out there.

The problem often isn't the Realist's actions but the intentions behind his actions: he'll do the right thing not for the sake of doing something good but because it makes him look good. He'll compromise in the relationship, but it'll be in such a way that favors him. To the Realist with a strong ego, all things rebound on him.

The Realist likes to test just how emotionally involved you are with him, so he'll do almost anything to get a reaction out of you. This is yet another consequence of his hubris: the more you give in to him emotionally, the more it strokes his ego. Writing entire novels to him that encompass your every feeling via text is not the way to win an argument with this archetype. If you do things like this, you surrender emotional power that you should be retaining for yourself. If you're having a disagreement with the Realist, it's wiser to respond to him with few words, because this will give him the impression that you don't care and that he needs to try harder (not to mention that it'll drive him crazy). Remember that the ego may be loud and proud, but it is also fearful. All in all, the Realist is a complex life path.

The Realist is brutally honest, which is the reason behind many of his disputes: he tells it like it is, even when people aren't ready to listen. In a relationship, he is likely to be honest with his partner no matter what—he'll even confess if he's fallen in love with another woman! If his partner betrays him, he'll lose trust quickly and often permanently. Be careful not to insult the Realist or play on his weaknesses; his ego can shift into overdrive and he may become sarcastic. He might overreact and reiterate some painful truths, after which he'll feel sorry for what he said and did. Even constructive criticism can be misconstrued by this life path; constantly telling the Realist he's "wrong" will do nothing to make him realize that he's wrong.

Voicing your dissatisfactions to a Realist is tricky because his ego can prevent him from seeing that he's doing anything wrong. He may get extremely defensive since confrontation rattles his reality. Express yourself gently to the Realist when discussing aspects about himself that he needs to change or improve. Reassure him of his strengths and what he's done right first. This archetype requires encouragement and compliments that make him feel worthy. It's pivotal to let the Realist win, but only up to a certain point. Once his complacency starts getting in your way or holding you back, it's time to address the issue.

The Realist will commit to the person who indulges him but who also indulges herself. Despite how much he relies on his ego, the Realist wants to see that his partner takes care of her needs too. The woman who chooses to be with a Realist cannot be a weak woman; you'll have to be as tough as the Realist is to keep up a relationship with him. Tending your own ambitions and desires will make the Realist see he's found his self-loving match.

COMPATIBILITY FOR THE REALIST

The Realist and the Independent (4 and 1)—likely to be in a compromise relationship: This combination can be a bit tricky, particularly because neither the Independent nor the Realist has ample patience for each other—they are notoriously headstrong. The Realist has patience for his assignments but not always for those around him, and the Independent has patience to implement his every whim. The 1 is quick to execute his ideas and follow through on his plans, but the 4 believes that planning is sometimes more important than doing. The Realist needs to be in control of all circumstances, including his relationships, but the last thing the Independent wants is to be controlled. This can lead to frequent clashes of energy between these two numbers. The Realist also wants a partner who will tend to his needs, but the Independent simply isn't willing to dedicate so much time and effort to another person. The dynamic of this relationship is more like an employer and employee: one gives careful instructions and the other puts them into action. What helps is that they're both highly pragmatic. As lovers, however, these life paths have numerous challenges to overcome because of their divergent personalities.

The Realist and the Introvert (4 and 2)—likely to be in a compromise relationship: The Introvert and Realist make a couple with potential but in need of work; this is a relationship in which sensitivity and sense mingle, where imagination and discipline meet. The 2 can offer the 4 the attention of which he's so needy, but he must first feel comfortable enough to be himself around his partner. This will take some patience on the part of the Realist, but it will be worth it. Both partners in this relationship are calculated and tactful, with the Introvert having the added bonus of superb intuition. He can guide the Realist when he's not seeing the bigger picture or stuck in a conundrum. In turn, the Realist will enjoy providing stability to his partner and meeting his significant other's every need. As down to earth as he is, the Realist will indulge in the Introvert's creativity and dreams for the future; the 2's prolific mind is like a breath of fresh air to the strict and rigid 4. He must take care not to be too inflexible, which can offend the Introvert. Both partners depend on themselves for answers, yet both can teach each other the value of seeking guidance from their other half when in need.

The Realist and the Extrovert (4 and 3)—likely to be in a toxic relationship: The main difference between these partners lies in the ways they approach decision-making. The Realist is pragmatic and tactful, ensuring he has control over all the variables before he proceeds. The Extrovert, on the other hand, likes to throw caution to the wind and dive headlong into choices that aren't always well calculated. If they're planning dinner, the 3 will want to go "wherever there's a good crowd," while the 4 will scour the restaurant's reviews, make reservations, and confirm them twice. Both these archetypes are concerned with their appearance, so an Extrovert and Realist couple can come across as vain if shallow tendencies aren't mitigated. It's necessary for these partners to learn the value of sacrificing for one another and the rewards that come with giving without expecting to receive. All in all, one balances the energy of the other. An Extrovert can show a Realist the beauty of human connections and letting loose once in a while, and a Realist can teach an Extrovert that careful planning ensures success. They make an excellent couple to work on a project: the Realist will set up the logistics and the Extrovert will handle publicity.

The Realist and the Realist (4 and 4)—likely to be in a compromise relationship: Two Realists can work as a couple, but each must make sure his personal needs are being met. Because the Realist is often caught up in his own thoughts, a 4-to-4 relationship can equal much silence and little expression. The Realists must learn to communicate—openly, honestly, and considering their partner's needs as much as they consider their own. They should help each other act, not only plan. Because the Realist wants his significant other to regard him as a positive force in his life, two of these personality types will try to outdo each other, both in good and bad ways; a competitive edge will always exist in this relationship that must be kept under control. There's also the possibility of each Realist becoming too serious and dry for his own good. If this happens, the relationship will lose its magic; it will become void of the wild dreams that every couple should share, even if they're sometimes a bit unrealistic. Passion can dwindle in the face of prudence if the 4s become too uptight. But if each partner learns how to let his proud guard down and use his imagination, two Realists can satisfy both themselves and their other half.

The Realist and the Free Spirit (4 and 5)—likely to be in a transitory relationship: It's difficult for a Realist and a Free Spirit to be in a relationship, because there will be more pulling them apart than keeping them together. The Realist needs someone to cater to him, but the Free Spirit has inherent problems with commitment. The Free Spirit might renege on his promises or dismiss his partner's requests, which will upset the Realist. Both put their own needs before their partner's, resulting in persistent discord and, if they're not careful, separation. Because Realists are missing a mental filter and prefer the raw truth to pleasing people, the 4 can easily wound the 5 with his words without intending to. It is not in the Free Spirit's nature to stick around through thick and thin; if he feels uncomfortable—even if it's for his own self-improvement—he'll move on. If this couple is determined to form a union, however, each of the life paths will have to learn his personal lessons first: the Realist must learn how to prioritize his partner, and the Free Spirit must learn how to be grounded. In other words, the Realist needs to esteem his significant other as much as he esteems himself, and the Free Spirit needs to honor the concept of a relationship as a whole.

The Realist and the Hopeless Romantic (4 and 6)—likely to be in a complementary relationship: The Hopeless Romantic lives to please, while the Realist enjoys being pleased. This relationship can last, but it might benefit one side more than the other, which will quickly become evident to friends and family. The Realist will let the Hopeless Romantic know exactly what he wants and needs without pretense. Subsequently, the Hopeless Romantic must learn how to do the same, or he won't get what he deserves out of this relationship. The Hopeless Romantic needs to put his foot down and speak up—to be honest when his partner isn't meting his expectations, and to ask the Realist to fulfill his wishes too. The good thing is that, in his own way, the Realist enjoys gratifying his other half, too. If the 6 can bring himself to ask, the 4 will provide. Because he wants a partner who takes good care of himself, the Realist will be enamored with a Hopeless Romantic who keeps up her image. The Hopeless Romantic can show the Realist how to cast aside his logic and dream a little. Both partners will be concerned with the appearance of their home and will put much effort into turning a house into a haven for their family.

The Realist and the Spiritual Seeker (4 and 7)—likely to be in a stagnant relationship: This can be an interesting match, with each partner broadening the mindset of the other. The Realist is a rational, no-nonsense kind of person, while the Spiritual Seeker has fascinating ideas about this world and beyond. What results is a relationship in which, if each partner respects the other's viewpoints, new perspectives about the world can be gained: the 4 will realize that magic lies beyond the science of reasoning, and the 7 can acknowledge that practicality is sometimes the only way to advance in the real world. The Spiritual Seeker, however, will not hesitate to explore other options should he see that the Realist isn't requiting his efforts. The Realist wants to provide for his partner, but he needs to be given a nudge in the right direction and be told what would be most helpful. The Spiritual Seeker may not be able to provide this information since he's so often locked away in his own mind, and, truth be told, the Realist is equally closed off, planning but seldom doing. What's required of both partners is to search for solutions when discrepancies become too broad. The absence of excitement will be palpable in this relationship more than in many others.

The Realist and the Workaholic (4 and 8)—likely to be in a karmic relationship: The Realist and Workaholic share core values that will help them remain together: loyalty, perseverance, and hard work are among the ideals these archetypes hold in high regard. They can build solid things owing to their principles, from a family to a business to a home. The Realist will lean on the Workaholic for little things, but the Workaholic will reject this tendency; he has a business to run and a career to attend to, and little time to resolve the minor inconveniences of his partner. The 8 appreciates when he's not bothered for every small matter, but the 4 wants to be aware of everything his partner is up to. One problem that might crop up is that the Workaholic doesn't have enough time to devote to the Realist, who is a needy archetype. When this happens, the Realist needs to address his concerns but also tend to his own goals. Stability is one of the key words that anchors these two life paths in reality and keeps them sane, and it is stability that can keep them thriving as a couple. When an earthquake strikes, such as a sudden loss or disaster, it can be hard for these numbers to regain firm ground. What the Realist and Workaholic must remember is to rely on each other to break through any adversity.

The Realist and the Well-Rounded One (4 and 9)—likely to be in a compromise relationship: These two life paths make excellent planners, with the 4 thinking in the short term and the 9 thinking for the long term. The Realist can learn valuable lessons from his evolved partner about wisdom and compassion, virtues that span beyond logic and information. Perhaps the greatest one will come from following in his partner's footsteps and turning his dreams into actual decisions. In terms of needs, the Realist will expect the Well-Rounded One to wait on him, but the Well-Rounded One will be more concerned with the salvation of others.

This is not to say the Well-Rounded One won't be sympathetic to the Realist; if there's one thing the Well-Rounded One has, it's empathy for those around him, in particular the partner he loves. Because the Well-Rounded One cares about the people in his life—as dysfunctional as they may be—the Realist must take care never to speak poorly of or insult his partner's family members. These are two intelligent archetypes, though one is more concerned with his own needs and the other with the needs of others. The 9 won't be impressed with the 4's conceitedness in the least. The Realist will have to be okay with the Well-Rounded One's concern for humanity and coming second for the sake of the greater good. If he is, then this couple can forge a way forward.

CHAPTER EIGHT

LIFE PATH 5: THE FREE SPIRIT

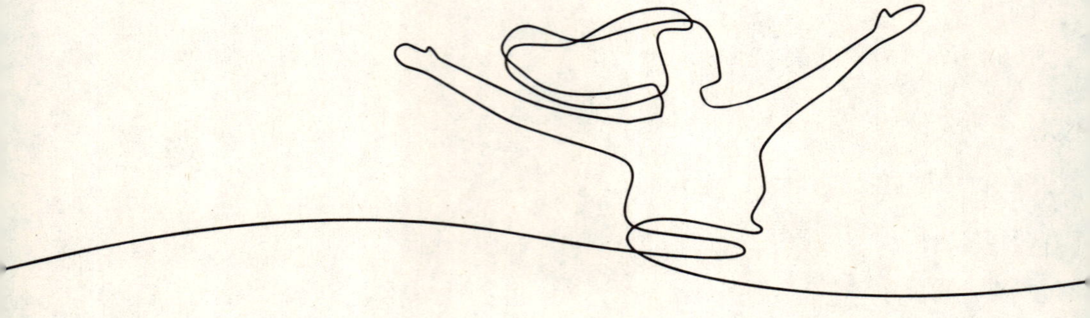

Count each day as a separate life.

—Seneca

THE FREE SPIRIT IS SYNONYMOUS WITH CARPE DIEM, a Latin phrase meaning "seize the day." Indeed, the Free Spirit wakes up to each day as though it were a new life. He is ready to celebrate at any moment, for any reason. The 5 has a highly individualistic attitude and likes to think of himself as a nonconformist: he enjoys going against trends and marching to the beat of a different drum. The Free Spirit needs constant stimulation of the five senses to feel satisfied. His word of choice is passion, and he sprinkles it on all he does. He should, however, be careful not to confuse passion with escape: it is one thing to be excited about traveling, and another to move from city to city to evade thoughts you can't process or memories you don't want to remember.

This archetype may claim he wants to have a relationship but jumps ship when things get serious. This can leave his significant other bemused and blaming herself when, in reality, the Free Spirit's problem is not his partner but the notion of commitment itself. The Free Spirit doesn't necessarily act on fear; he simply finds it hard to stay still, both literally and figuratively, and likes to experiment with different things while getting attached to none. If there's one thing the Free Spirit would like to be doing, it's waking up in a new part of the world each week and going on adventures every day. Members of this life path, like Extroverts, place a heavy emphasis on the way they appear to others and like to look their best at all times.

The 5 needs to remain in control of his circumstances. He believes that if he gets attached, whether it's to a partner, job, or location, he'll lose control. He cannot allow a person, belief system, or institution to have authority over him. Thus, the Free Spirit comes across as curiously detached from material possessions, society, religion, and even his family members. This may be because the Free Spirit hasn't secured a sense of self, despite his age. Even in his 30s, 40s, and beyond, the Free Spirit hasn't yet discovered who he is or what he stands for. As you can imagine, this erects a significant hurdle in his love relationships.

Unlike with the Realist, stability is a challenge to achieve for the Free Spirit. He is impulsive, taking risks and acting on the emotions he feels at the time. He hasn't organized his thoughts and emotions adequately to follow through on one way of thinking and doing. In the heat of the moment, the Free Spirit might tell you that he loves you, but when he leaves your house, the love he just professed leaves as well. Once he sees the effort that's going to be required of him, he retracts from the relationship. The moment he gets too comfortable anywhere, this life path uproots himself for reasons known only to him.

The Free Spirit is transient in his emotions and elusive in his nature, flitting between wanting a partner and wanting to wander. He can't choose between one or the other, so he wants both. He conveniently fails to recognize that relationships don't work that way. His presence can be ephemeral, coming on strongly and then disappearing for several days straight or turning into a seemingly different person overnight. The 5 also says one thing and then does another, making promises he sometimes can't keep. Trying to talk sense into this life path is a dead-end road; you would have more luck making your cat understand why you should get married. If an argument is bad enough, it can trigger a switch in the Free Spirit and shift his intentions. It'll make him revisit everything he believes, then pack his things and leave. When the going gets tough, the tough get going . . . right out the front door, along with the Free Spirit.

The Free Spirit can have bona fide feelings for his partner, but he doesn't know how to hold on to them for long enough. He therefore loses the momentum needed to pull through on his intentions. He bounces around, losing interest and going from conviction to confusion quickly. He can be an emotional nomad, roving around in his feelings without settling on one. This archetype is able to juggle multiple relationships at once without letting any advance too far. Whereas some people can have two partners and be seriously involved with both, the Free Spirit doesn't become emotionally intimate with any of his love interests. We can presume this to be incredibly frustrating for the person who genuinely likes a Free Spirit.

Despite his attachment issues, the Free Spirit is a "people person." He can mingle for hours on end and charm almost anyone, things an Introvert would find exhausting. This primary number has sympathy for others and enjoys giving; when it comes to charity, he'll donate a generous amount without a second thought. The reason for this may be that he's not attached to the notion of money like most people.

The Free Spirit views life through a broader perspective, almost like an outsider, and acknowledges the pros and cons of anything. Through the Free Spirit's mind pass all possibilities with equal conviction. The Free Spirit recognizes potential in everything, so he does see the potential of being in a relationship with a person he likes, but he falls short of taking the right actions. He feels a torrent of emotions that can be overwhelming. He wants to accomplish everything at once but ends up accomplishing nothing or very little. Many people don't have the time or patience to devote to a person who commits halfway, and some partners automatically assume the Free Spirit is out to hurt them. The truth is that this life path only hurts himself by being so unsettled: he sabotages his own chances of success, happiness, and progress by not staying on track. He is capable of mutability and evolution, but he needs an extra shove in climbing the next rung on the ladder. There is hope for this life path, as there is for anyone who wants to change.

If the Free Spirit does fear anything, it's failure. He doesn't like to put effort into achieving something, whether it's a long-term relationship or successful career, because it might not work out. Here, his underdeveloped sense of self becomes evident: goals seem intimidating to the Free Spirit because he doesn't believe enough in himself. In contrast to the Well-Rounded One, he handles responsibilities poorly and prefers to run away rather than mitigate issues. But the Free Spirit doesn't want to remain undecided all his life; we all are hardwired for stability. Putting intention into action is where the Free Spirit gets stuck. He can give his partner something solid only once he's solid in himself, but he must first discover what he stands for. This number needs to build a strong sense of self and underline his life values. He has to learn how to commit seriously to his ambitions before he can commit to a love relationship. A patient partner will be the Free Spirit's lifeline to reach stability.

One thing she can do for the Free Spirit is help him condense his thoughts and manage conflictual tendencies so that he learns how to allow his emotions to come and go without always acting on them. Setting attainable aims for the 5 and assisting him in completing them helps, as does encouraging him to carve one path for himself and stay on it. The Free Spirit should be reminded of how rewarding it is to be dedicated to something, and to see it through to the end instead of walking away when monotony strikes. The more he learns how to stick to one job, project, or belief, the more likely the Free Spirit is to stick to one relationship. To prevail in his personal undertakings, the Free Spirit will have to embed himself in one area of life, then another, then another. Once he's grounded in purpose, the Free Spirit can finally commit to a partner. This archetype reminds us why self-knowledge is paramount in understanding who we are, what we want, and what we can offer another person.

COMPATIBILITY FOR THE FREE SPIRIT

The Free Spirit and the Independent (5 and 1)—likely to be in a stagnant relationship: If ever there was a couple that values freedom, the Independent and Free Spirit is it. Both the 1 and 5 want time apart from each other; they need space to make it work. These are not exactly needy numbers desperate to curl into each other's arms every night; they're fine not seeing each other for a week (or two) and simply checking in once a day. The Independent wants to focus on his ambitions, and the Free Spirit wants to travel and go on adventures. Each will take comfort in the fact that, when all is said and done, there's someone there for him. This kind of relationship, unfortunately, can lead to detachment and easy breakups. They have to be careful not to become too detached from one another, since each archetype can easily become absorbed in his own world; I've seen 1s and 5s fizzle out not because of underlying problems within the relationship, but because both partners simply lived separate lives. These numbers can have trouble settling down after years of dating, and their families might start to ask, "When are you getting married? Are you ever going to have children?" Neither will know how to answer such questions, or if there is a right answer at all. When the Independent and Free Spirit do reunite after a break, their enthusiasm will be palpable and their romance will be at its peak. If each partner can live with the other while living apart, this relationship is sustainable.

The Free Spirit and the Introvert (5 and 2)—likely to be in a compromise relationship: This relationship requires work. The Introvert will want to stay home and curl up with a good book, which the Free Spirit will find terribly boring. The Free Spirit craves action and adventure, something the Introvert rarely desires. In fact, too much commotion leaves the Introvert emotionally drained. It has the opposite effect on the Free Spirit, recharging his batteries and amplifying his energy. The Free Spirit will take the liberty to plan the couple's copious activities, which the Introvert won't exactly look forward to, since he holds sacred the comfort of his home. The Introvert needs deep intellectual stimulation to feel satisfied, but the Free Spirit just wants to explore and experience different things. The 2 will try to share his sentiments with the 5, but the Free Spirit might not always understand the breadth of his partner's feelings. It is crucial for the Introvert to refrain from pushing the Free Spirit's buttons or infringing upon his liberties, and it's equally important for the Free Spirit to put effort into getting to know the Introvert truly and deeply. If the Free Spirit doesn't inspire trust in the Introvert, their relationship will simply dissolve. These two numbers must share at least some core values if they want to survive as a couple.

The Free Spirit and the Extrovert (5 and 3)—likely to be in a transitory relationship: Spontaneity spells out the union between these partners, who are ready to pack their bags and travel across the world on a whim. Both tend to dive into their decisions, yes, but the Extrovert knows a limit to the risks he takes, whereas the Free Spirit does not. The 5 is not just friendly and sociable—he can be downright reckless, which is something the 3 is not. The Free Spirit's indecisiveness will affect this relationship (as it does all areas of his life), and his inability to commit will turn off the Extrovert, who is perfectly capable of being in a serious relationship in spite of his outgoing personality. The moment the Extrovert becomes judgmental of his partner and gives him a piece of his mind, the Free Spirit might reconsider the relationship, collect his belongings, and leave. The Extrovert will waste no time in finding a replacement, which is not the right approach either. There is a desperate demand for heartfelt communication between these numbers, and a need to learn how to navigate through rough waters instead of abandoning ship. On a lighter note, you can be sure that an Extrovert and a Free Spirit will steal the spotlight the moment they waltz into a party together.

The Free Spirit and the Realist (5 and 4)—likely to be in a transitory relationship: It's difficult for a Realist and a Free Spirit to be in a relationship, because there will be more pulling them apart than keeping them together. The Realist needs someone to cater to him, but the Free Spirit has inherent problems with commitment. The Free Spirit might renege on his promises or dismiss his partner's requests, which will upset the Realist. Both put their own needs before their partner's, resulting in persistent discord and, if they're not careful, separation. Because Realists are missing a mental filter and prefer the raw truth to pleasing people, the 4 can easily wound the 5 with his words without intending to. It is not in the Free Spirit's nature to stick around through thick and thin; if he feels uncomfortable—even if it's for his own self-improvement—he'll move on. If this couple is determined to form a union, however, each of the life paths will have to learn his personal lessons first: the Realist must learn how to prioritize his partner, and the Free Spirit must learn how to be grounded. In other words, the Realist needs to esteem his significant other as much as he esteems himself, and the Free Spirit needs to honor the concept of a relationship as a whole.

The Free Spirit and the Free Spirit (5 and 5)—likely to be in a transitory relationship: This relationship is like an unscripted movie in which the actors are improvising as they go along. It's unknown what twists and turns the movie will take or how it will end. The Free Spirit is the embodiment of spontaneity, and when you put two Free Spirits together, it's highly likely that chaos will ensue (or something explodes). A 5 means well, but he can't bring himself to carry out his promises. This means that one or both partners will often feel disappointed. The Free Spirit couple would do well to keep matters private and not allow external forces to influence them, such as friends and family who aren't exactly in favor of the relationship. As an archetype, the Free Spirit must be taught how to slow down and stay in one place, grounding himself by performing work that's meaningful to him. But who will teach him these lessons, if his partner is just as reckless? Two Free Spirits can take off like two rockets in opposite directions. When one thing goes wrong, they might look at each other and simultaneously say, "This isn't going to work." If they're living on the less evolved side of their life paths, the 5s will move on to their next romances without having learned anything. On the upside, physical intercourse between these partners is mind blowing, and two Free Spirits make a stellar traveling couple, ready to board a plane, ship, or spacecraft on a moment's notice.

The Free Spirit and the Hopeless Romantic (5 and 6)—likely to be in a toxic relationship: One of the archetypes who can ground the Free Spirit and help him reach stability is the Hopeless Romantic. Granted, it will be no easy feat, but the Hopeless Romantic is ready to take up the work to convert the Free Spirit into a docile, loyal partner. The 6 has the patience of a saint, which is exactly what's needed to help the 5 go from nomad to homebody. There will be setbacks, of course, since the Free Spirit is one of the more difficult archetypes to work with. But the Free Spirit will be grateful for the Hopeless Romantic's sacrifice, which should inspire the Free Spirit to work on such character traits in himself. The Hopeless Romantic should be cautious not to invest himself to the point of exhaustion and neglect his own needs, or he'll experience overwhelming disappointment. The Hopeless Romantic is overly caring and sensitive, and if he sees that the Free Spirit isn't settling down at the rate he expects, he might become frustrated and hurt. At their best, these partners can settle down in a real relationship and be equally devoted to one another. At their worst, the Free Spirit will resist the Hopeless Romantic's efforts and abuse his partner's generosity.

The Free Spirit and the Spiritual Seeker (5 and 7)—likely to be in a stagnant relationship: The Free Spirit will be impressed by the Spiritual Seeker's unique take on the world and wealth of knowledge. The Spiritual Seeker will like that the Free Spirit can give him time alone. This couple gets great joy out of traveling together, the Spiritual Seeker to expand his knowledge of other cultures and belief systems and the Free Spirit for the sheer thrill of it. The problem, again, comes from the Free Spirit's inability to get attached for too long. The Spiritual Seeker will have to learn to tame the Free Spirit's wild side, or he'll be in for some unpleasant surprises: the 5 has a terrible tendency to vanish when things get tough. The Spiritual Seeker is just as free spirited as his partner, but he is able to commit to one person for the long run. The Free Spirit is more concerned with sensual pleasures, while the Spiritual Seeker wants to achieve serenity of the soul. In the true nature of a Spiritual Seeker, this archetype will try to analyze the Free Spirit in an attempt to figure him out. It is wise for these partners not to engage in verbal confrontation, since the 7 can be careless with his words and devastate the 5. This couple should work on their mutual interests and take every day as it comes, with each partner embracing the joys that his significant other can introduce into his life.

The Free Spirit and the Workaholic (5 and 8)—likely to be in a compromise relationship: Both these archetypes are energetic and animated, but not both can apply themselves thoroughly to their goals; only the Workaholic can do that. Under no circumstances will the 8 chase someone. The Workaholic will not put his work on pause to catch the runaway Free Spirit and tug him by the ear back to his relationship. He simply doesn't have time for that. Instead, he'll let the Free Spirit walk out the door if that's what he chooses to do. The Free Spirit, as we know, is not likely to settle down of his own accord unless his partner teaches him the merits of monogamy. The Free Spirit can be instrumental in aiding the Workaholic if he finds his partner's work interesting; he will gladly travel and meet with people on behalf of the Workaholic. Interestingly, both the 5 and 8 enjoy the finer things in life and splurge without glancing at the bill. One thing the Workaholic will appreciate is that the Free Spirit will give him the space he needs to tend to his career. The Free Spirit won't be on top of the Workaholic for every little thing, which would be a deal-breaker to the Workaholic. If the Free Spirit can settle down with a Workaholic without acting on that sudden whim to leave, these two life paths will call themselves a couple for a long time.

The Free Spirit and the Well-Rounded One (5 and 9)—likely to be in a complementary relationship: This is a relationship in which both partners allow each other to be themselves. The Well-Rounded One does not seek to alter the Free Spirit, as other archetypes do; instead, he invites the Free Spirit to express himself. The Free Spirit wishes to support the Well-Rounded One in his most noble endeavors, from starting a charity to opening a chain of shelters. This couple will love to travel, the Free Spirit to have new experiences and the Well-Rounded One to scope out areas where he can help those in need. But if the Well-Rounded One gets attached and the Free Spirit isn't completely convinced of his intentions, he risks being seriously hurt by the 5. The Well-Rounded One is loving but also realistic; he probably won't allow the Free Spirit a second chance, because he's wise enough to know that what his partner did once, he will do again. If the Well-Rounded One feels that the Free Spirit can't give him a serious relationship, he won't waste time trying to convince him otherwise. The best thing the 9 can do for the 5 is to help him settle down physically and emotionally so that their relationship has the greatest chances of success. In terms of chemistry, the Well-Rounded One will be instantly attracted to the Free Spirit's irresistible charm. The Free Spirit will savor the attention and get sucked in right away.

CHAPTER NINE

LIFE PATH 6: THE HOPELESS ROMANTIC

One word frees us of all the
weight and pain in life.
That word is love.

—Sophocles

THE HOPELESS ROMANTIC BELIEVES THAT LOVE is the only reward one can call his own. In literature, these life paths are depicted as characters who revere love more than life itself. They're usually protagonists who sacrifice their own lives to save the one they love from mortal peril. The real-world Hopeless Romantic is not much different: he bursts into a relationship like a medieval knight charges into battle, ready to risk it all for the maiden's hand in marriage. Number 6 is on a constant, quixotic quest to secure a life partner. His theory is not wrong, but his strategy is: the Hopeless Romantic is the kind of person who proposes one month after meeting his partner, rushing things and not thinking them through for the sake of having a relationship. His wholehearted belief in love is admirable, but it can make him aimless and tactless. This number can become blemished by exaggerated love, throwing himself into relationships blindly or falling in love with the wrong person altogether.

If you're on the receiving end of a relationship with a Hopeless Romantic, you might feel overwhelmed: he will come on strongly and be needy of your time and attention. If you don't reciprocate these gestures, the Hopeless Romantic will get offended and take it personally. Rather than taking a step back and trying to be more gentle, number 6 will come on even more strongly. He might try to impose on your life, thinking he's doing you a favor or showing you the right way to do things. This life path is on a mission to "save" his partner, trying to improve her life in any way possible. He might have the best of intentions, but his approach intimidates and even scares away many of his love interests. Although it becomes evident that he's harmless, a Hopeless Romantic's insistence is likely to turn off even the most tolerant partner. It's possible that the Hopeless Romantic subconsciously struggles with feelings of inadequacy and is trying to make up for self-perceived failings by working extra hard in his relationship. This archetype argues that the more effort he puts into his relationship, the less likely his partner is to leave him. If he's vibrating at a low frequency, he can turn jealous, possessive, and domineering.

The Hopeless Romantic has a propensity for self-harm, especially when he's hurting in love. He can't come to terms with a failing relationship or a partner who did him wrong. There's no coping with a breakup the normal way for a 6; he must do something extreme to help him forget, such as drinking or sleeping around or moving to a different part of the world. When they suffer from a broken heart, Hopeless Romantics feel as if the world has come to a halt. They have an obsessive personality that can turn self-destructive if they're not keeping busy with positive, productive activities.

Hopeless Romantics aren't easily discouraged and are predisposed to see the good in their partners, whether that good exists or not. Being a Hopeless Romantic alters the way one views relationships in unrealistic ways. This life path might be setting himself up for failure by having unreasonable expectations in a relationship, but he also has a more positive opinion of his partner overall; he might make excuses for his significant other or make himself believe that she's meeting his expectations when in reality she's not. Those who uphold romantic beliefs about their relationship seem to be more satisfied in their relationships, but they also may be deluding themselves into false beliefs. The Hopeless Romantic is a people pleaser, or rather, a partner pleaser. He is inherently noble and thrives when he's doing good for others, especially the person he loves most. If this life path is able to step back and view his relationship in more-realistic terms, he can make sound decisions that benefit both him and his loved one.

If he's not able to curb his enthusiasm, the Hopeless Romantic can become reckless just to please his partner; this is, after all, his tragic flaw. The Hopeless Romantic can lose touch with reality if he's too set on reaching ideal love. He yearns for commitment but doesn't know how to approach it in a thoughtful, calculated way. A 6 will fall so head over heels in love he won't realize that his partner is actually an awful person. He takes all that his other half says at face value, so you can imagine that it's not too difficult to lie to a Hopeless Romantic who's in love with you.

The definition of a daydreamer, this number remains blind to the truth by choice; this is the type of partner who, despite evidence, refuses to believe that the person he loves is cheating on or lying to him. He may forgive his partner one too many times and return again and again to identical scenarios, convinced that they'll end differently this time.

Cognitive dissonance is a state of mind in which we willfully choose to do something we know is harmful to us or others. This life path can live in a permanent state of cognitive dissonance, making decisions that are inconsistent with reality. The Hopeless Romantic is often guilty of cognitive dissonance, knowing that his partner isn't good for him yet choosing to stay in the relationship. His notion of love is so grand that he sees it as a panacea: he sincerely believes that if he loves hard enough, love will fix all his problems.

The Hopeless Romantic is aware when he's at fault, and he usually assumes responsibility for wrong actions. This number will put aside his ego and try to make things up to his loved one. He has no hidden motives; he just wants to give and receive love and has been ready to commit himself fully to another person for quite some time. This archetype tends to be infatuated with one person at a time, which is why he's unlikely to cheat. Those born under this life path don't betray; they get betrayed (if they do betray, it's because they've been betrayed and turned vengeful as a result of vibrating at a low frequency).

What ends up happening is that the Hopeless Romantic repeatedly attracts partners who can't requite his efforts, whether physically, emotionally, or mentally. It's important for the 6 not to get stuck in a one-sided relationship, because he won't be able to let go easily and will cause himself undue pain. He'll put much effort into forcing his partner to commit when she may not want or be able to. It takes a lot to break down the Hopeless Romantic's passion for his partner. But when the walls do come crashing down, no one experiences disappointment more severely than a 6, who portrays himself as a victim when his partner has let him down. And when push comes to shove, this life path will begrudgingly remind his partner how much he did (and probably paid) for her. As a harsh reality sets in, the 6 might experience a cascade of nightmarish thoughts, from bitterness and resentment to rage and contempt. Being let down causes the Hopeless Romantic to become cynical in future relationships.

The Hopeless Romantic needs a home he feels good in. A comfortable and cozy interior setting is vital to this life path, providing him with emotional stability and peace of mind. Male or female, the Hopeless Romantic takes great pride in his home, whether it's a studio apartment or a villa. A 6 will spare no expense in decorating his home and fixing whatever is necessary. He feels even more fulfilled when his space is filled with children playing and family members laughing; he craves the warmth of a close-knit family. This is a highly nurturing archetype, so it follows naturally that he wants kids to raise and care for. Even if he chooses not to have children, the Hopeless Romantic will treat the people in his life like family.

When he's not concentrated on love, the Hopeless Romantic's brain is roving over different ideas—goals he would like to implement for himself. But without some help, they remain in the contents of his mind, and when he meets opposition to one, he swiftly moves on to the next.

Unlike the Introvert, the Hopeless Romantic doesn't have communication impediments. He is completely open and wears his heart on his sleeve. To keep up a durable relationship with this primary number, his partner will have to teach him how to exercise practicality and reasonable expectations. It's helpful for the 6's partner to take the reins by setting healthful boundaries without hurting his feelings. In this way, he can learn how to put himself first and not sacrifice without end for his significant other, especially when it's not necessary. It brings joy to the Hopeless Romantic to do things for his partner, but he must be stopped from going overboard or exhausting himself. This life path is happiest when he's bringing a smile to his loved one's face, but he deserves equal attention in return. He fares well with a partner who anchors him down and takes control in a responsible way, reminding him that she'll love him no less if he considers his needs too. If the Hopeless Romantic can comprehend that slow progress is true progress, then he can have the relationship he's always dreamed of.

COMPATIBILITY FOR THE HOPELESS ROMANTIC

The Hopeless Romantic and the Independent (6 and 1)—likely to be in a toxic relationship: The problem with this couple isn't that they aren't compatible, it's that one partner will try to do too much for the other. Because the Hopeless Romantic is naturally generous and nurturing, he will try to shower the Independent with attention, which the Independent won't want to accept. Coming on too strongly is a prime way to scare off an Independent, but the Hopeless Romantic won't be deterred one bit; he'll simply push harder. This game of tug-of-war won't lead to a successful relationship. The 1 and 6 partners must learn how to compromise: the Hopeless Romantic will have to grant the Independent his personal space when he needs it, and the Independent will have to allow the Hopeless Romantic to care for him to a certain degree. Both the Hopeless Romantic and Independent will try to do things their way because it is in their characters to get things done, often on their own. These numbers fail to realize that in a relationship, cooperation is key to success. For this pair to work, each partner will have to perform his duties without overstepping the boundaries of the other, and to praise his significant other for his excellent work.

The Hopeless Romantic and the Introvert (6 and 2)—likely to be in a soulmate relationship: This is a couple that can last a lifetime. They share many essential elements in common, such as comfort, compassion, and the ideal of family. The Introvert wants a partner he can trust, while the Hopeless Romantic wants to prove his trustworthiness to his partner: they fit like hand and glove. The Hopeless Romantic must remember not to overindulge the Introvert and to allow him time alone so that the 2 can reflect on his emotions and reenergize himself, and the Introvert needs to reassure the Hopeless Romantic that he's doing a great job of making him happy. Together, they can work magic around the house, adding personal touches around every corner. These archetypes don't like surprises; they appreciate predictability above all and seek it in each other. Few things hurt them more than suffering disappointment at the hands of the person they love, so each has learned the importance of not letting his significant other down. The Hopeless Romantic will put the Introvert at the center of his world and do everything in his power to please him. The Introvert will sense his good intentions and welcome the Hopeless Romantic into his imaginative world.

The Hopeless Romantic and the Extrovert (6 and 3)—likely to be in a compromise relationship: This relationship abounds with passion . . . of two different kinds: the Extrovert's passion for life and the Hopeless Romantic's passion for his partner. The Hopeless Romantic will embolden the Extrovert in all his endeavors, whether they are wise or foolish. In return, the Extrovert will give the Hopeless Romantic plenty of attention. But when one partner does not feel adequately cared for in this relationship, their discrepancies become pronounced: if the 6 does not feel appreciated, he will push harder for his partner to recognize his efforts. If the 3 feels undervalued (which is unlikely, since the Hopeless Romantic lives to please), he might seek attention elsewhere. If the Extrovert is the one to lose interest, the Hopeless Romantic is unlikely to relinquish him, and the relationship can turn into a chasing game. The relationship doesn't have to reach this point if the partners find new ways of feeding their fervor for one another. The Extrovert will feel excited to return to a comfortable and beautifully decorated home, courtesy of the Hopeless Romantic, every night.

The Hopeless Romantic and the Realist (6 and 4)—likely to be in a complementary relationship: The Hopeless Romantic lives to please, while the Realist enjoys being pleased. This relationship can last, but it might benefit one side more than the other, which will quickly become evident to friends and family. The Realist will let the Hopeless Romantic know exactly what he wants and needs without pretense. Subsequently, the Hopeless Romantic must learn how to do the same, or he won't get what he deserves out of this relationship. The Hopeless Romantic needs to put his foot down and speak up—to be honest when his partner isn't meting his expectations and ask the Realist to fulfill his wishes too. The good thing is that, in his own way, the Realist enjoys gratifying his other half too. If the 6 can bring himself to ask, the 4 will provide. Because he wants a partner who takes good care of himself, the Realist will be enamored with a Hopeless Romantic who keeps up her image. The Hopeless Romantic can show the Realist how to cast aside his logic and dream a little. Both partners will be concerned with the appearance of their home and will put much effort into turning a house into a haven for their family.

The Hopeless Romantic and the Free Spirit (6 and 5)—likely to be in a toxic relationship: One of the archetypes who can ground the Free Spirit and help him reach stability is the Hopeless Romantic. Granted, it will be no easy feat, but the Hopeless Romantic is ready to take up the work to convert the Free Spirit into a docile, loyal partner. The 6 has the patience of a saint, which is exactly what's needed to help the 5 go from nomad to homebody. There will be setbacks, of course, since the Free Spirit is one of the more difficult archetypes to work with. But the Free Spirit will be grateful for the Hopeless Romantic's sacrifice, which should inspire the Free Spirit to work on such character traits in himself. The Hopeless Romantic should be cautious not to invest himself to the point of exhaustion and neglect his own needs, or he'll experience overwhelming disappointment. The Hopeless Romantic is overly caring and sensitive, and if he sees that the Free Spirit isn't settling down at the rate he expects, he might become frustrated and hurt. At their best, these partners can settle down in a real relationship and be equally devoted to one another. At their worst, the Free Spirit will resist the Hopeless Romantic's efforts and abuse his partner's generosity.

The Hopeless Romantic and the Hopeless Romantic (6 and 6)—likely to be in a soulmate relationship: Two Hopeless Romantics will spend their days trying to please each other; making their partner happy makes them happy. Perhaps their biggest issue is that they'll try to outdo each other in this sense, which isn't always a good thing. The 6s will live in a state of competition, each vying to be the better partner. While there should be mutual effort in a relationship, exaggerated sacrifice is counterproductive; it distracts the partners from more-important goals they could be manifesting, such as planning for the future or building together. One of the Hopeless Romantic's lessons in life is to learn how to be more grounded and realistic.

But if his partner is as starry eyed as he is, how will he learn this? Hopeless Romantics are notoriously quixotic, and two of these archetypes will live in a perpetual dreamland. One of their most negative tendencies is thinking the worst, so they might constantly doubt each other, often without reason. A much more positive aspect is that they'll be deeply in love with and devoted to one another for many years up to a lifetime.

The Hopeless Romantic and the Spiritual Seeker (6 and 7)—likely to be in a transitory relationship: The Hopeless Romantic will be eager to sip from the Spiritual Seeker's fountain of knowledge, and the Spiritual Seeker will hold the cup steady for his thirsty partner. But the 6 will also have to learn to give the 7 the alone time he needs to do his research, deliberate, and regenerate his mind. Otherwise, the Spiritual Seeker might feel that the Hopeless Romantic is draining him of energy, and won't want to continue in a relationship in which he's being suffocated. This couple is passionate in the bedroom and should work on inventing new ways of pleasing each other. The Spiritual Seeker will selflessly encourage the Hopeless Romantic not to pay so much attention to him but to hone his own talents and skills; 7s wholeheartedly believe that each person should fulfill his purpose on Earth. If there is an archetype that can suppress the Hopeless Romantic's overgiving tendencies, it is the Spiritual Seeker, who will reassure his partner that he's entirely able to take care of himself and has no problem coming second to the Hopeless Romantic's vocation.

The Hopeless Romantic and the Workaholic (6 and 8)—likely to be in a complementary relationship: This relationship can work, especially in regard to the Hopeless Romantic aiding the Workaholic in his work duties. The Hopeless Romantic will feel important every time the Workaholic assigns him a task, and will set out to execute it at once. That said, the Workaholic also has to take care not to treat his partner like an assistant, and to remind himself that his other half is his equal, not the hired help. If the Hopeless Romantic is neglected by the Workaholic, he will feel hurt and push harder. This may irritate the Workaholic, who just wants to get his work done in peace and doesn't want to be asked, "What can I do for you?" several times a day. If the 8 mistreats the 6, the Hopeless Romantic will retreat into a world of doubt and self-blame, knowing it was "too good" to be true. A rebuffed 6 can even stray outside the relationship: if his partner's love and affection don't suffice, the Hopeless Romantic can turn his attention elsewhere and become infatuated with someone else. The Workaholic will think his partner is being ungrateful, especially if he provides financial aid to the Hopeless Romantic.

The Hopeless Romantic and the Well-Rounded One (6 and 9)—likely to be in a soulmate relationship: The sky's the limit for this match. The Hopeless Romantic will first be drawn to the Well-Rounded One's discipline and advanced sense of morality, and the Well-Rounded One to the Hopeless Romantic's pure and bold heart. The Hopeless Romantic's mind is rife with lofty ideas that he has trouble externalizing in the real world; they remain in the Hopeless Romantic's mind, and when he meets opposition to one, he swiftly moves on to the next. Thankfully, the Well-Rounded One can teach the Hopeless Romantic the patience and practicality that's needed to bring a dream to fruition. No life path can ground the Hopeless Romantic and persuade him to materialize his goals more than the Well-Rounded One, whose compassion is infinite. Under the auspices of the Well-Rounded One, the Hopeless Romantic's full potential can bloom. The 9's sense of fairness also means he won't take advantage of his sacrificial 6 partner; he'll gently stop the Hopeless Romantic from overexerting himself in the relationship. In turn, the Hopeless Romantic will gift the Well-Rounded One with unconditional love and remain by his side under any circumstances. Only if they're living at low levels will they succumb to thinking the worst about each other.

CHAPTER TEN

LIFE PATH 7: THE SPIRITUAL SEEKER

Of all our possessions,
wisdom alone is immortal.

—Isokrates

THE SPIRITUAL SEEKER BELIEVES THAT WISDOM ALONE can take him beyond the mortal realm; he realizes that wisdom survives after the physical body expires. Number 7 is guided by spiritual principles; hence his name. If the Spiritual Seeker could ask only two questions throughout his life, they would be "Why?" and "What?" *Why* are we here? *What* happens after we die? Such is the nature of the Spiritual Seeker: to explore unconventional, philosophical, and metaphysical ideas about this world and beyond. This archetype seeks to hold the secrets of the universe in the palm of his hand. To him, there is no greater power than knowledge.

The number 7 carries special connotations in many cultures and religions: the seven days of creation in Judaism, the seven deadly sins in Christianity, the seven gates of hell in Islam, and the seven higher and lower worlds in Hinduism. Perhaps it is this sacred connection that lends the Spiritual Seeker his innate psychic abilities and keen perception of human nature.

The Spiritual Seeker lives with one foot metaphorically on the other side. He is highly interested in the paranormal elements of life, ones that science can't quite explain. Beyond being interested in them, this archetype wishes to assimilate them. The Spiritual Seeker wants to evolve and elevate, eventually reaching nirvana, moksha, or whatever he deems the state of soulful freedom to be. His soul wants to live out its earthly chapter profoundly and purposefully. To him, heaven and Earth are not separate; he believes we're meant to align with the divine while transitioning through this ephemeral human disguise. This endows the Spiritual Seeker with a powerful presence and a radiant aura; the 7's energy is palpable before he enters the room. He commands attention without even meaning to; when he speaks, others stop in their tracks because he conveys words of tremendous insight.

This life path can do well in a relationship if he has a partner who fuels his thirst for otherworldly knowledge. He won't be impressed by a person who's mundane, disinterested, superficial, or overly logical. He needs a partner who pursues the same amount of soulful stimulation. If he's in a relationship with a simpleminded person, the Spiritual Seeker will quickly become bored and look for an exit sign. Because he views life through a wider lens, the Spiritual Seeker won't waste time with a person who doesn't contribute to his evolution. He believes that staying in a transitory, toxic, stagnant, or compromise relationship stunts spiritual growth and burdens the soul with extra karma. The Spiritual Seeker needs a philosopher with whom he can hold deeply meaningful dialogues. Expect your Spiritual Seeker to be wholly faithful to you, since he's not impressed by dishonesty in the least.

Though he might not mean to, the Spiritual Seeker doesn't always make his partner feel appreciated or worthy. He is forthright and honest but sometimes has trouble articulating his adoration for his partner. And when he's not fond of someone, the Spiritual Seeker's dislike will cut through the air like a knife. If your relationship with a Spiritual Seeker comes to an end, you will find it more difficult to reconcile with him than any of the other archetypes; this life path means what he says and says what he means. When he closes a door, he locks it and throws away the key, convincing himself that it wasn't meant to be according to the greater plan.

The Spiritual Seeker will dive into his work if it piques his curiosity. He will become ardent about his career if it pervades the deeper layers of his mind and brings him the promise of knowledge and enlightenment. The 7 won't feel content being confined to an ordinary life. If he works a regular, day-to-day job, the Spiritual Seeker's mind will be elsewhere. He will liven up the workplace with acumen and existential questions. I once had a pedicurist who fit this description. One of the first things he asked me as he was starting my treatment was "Do you believe in past lives?" I quickly answered yes, and he proceeded to tell me all about his former reincarnations on Earth. Toward the end of my pedicure, I asked him his birthday, and, sure enough, he turned out to be a life path 7. One of the most interesting things he told me was "Most people think that because I give pedicures, I'm not a wise man. Then I surprise them when I start to talk." He certainly did surprise me, and our conversation confirmed that the Spiritual Seeker likes to inject a little bit of the "otherworld" into everyday life.

One aspect that's indispensable to the Spiritual Seeker is faith. This is the motive behind his curiosity: to find and root himself in a faithful base. This archetype needs to build conviction in something in order to feel complete. His mission is to ground himself in one system of beliefs so that he feels stable. Faith reinforces his purpose.

In case he doesn't find a spiritual outlet into which to pour his overabundance of energy, the Spiritual Seeker can turn reckless. The 7 who isn't rooted in faith can easily turn to sex, drugs, or alcohol for entertainment. While he realizes that none of these activities bring him true fulfillment, he at least releases some energy through them. A faithless 7 can become tiresome to have around, turning cynical and depleting others of energy.

The Spiritual Seeker's mind is filled with thoughts that can overwhelm him; he is bright and intellectual but also intense. He overanalyzes situations and contends with his own ideas at times. For example, he finds it unsettling if he starts thinking about reincarnation but can't find a theory that resonates with him. The Spiritual Seeker will take an idea and turn it every which way until he understands every facet of it—then he'll do it again just to make sure he hasn't missed anything. You can imagine how exhausting this is, not only to this archetype but also to the people around him. Like the Introvert, the Spiritual Seeker notices minute details and tiny features that others easily overlook. Members of this life path make excellent detectives, forensic scientists, and technical experts. Answers come to Spiritual Seekers almost instinctively, intuitively, as though from the divine.

Comparable to the Introvert, the Spiritual Seeker needs his space. He means this as no offense to his partner, but he's simply not an archetype in desperate need of attention. When the Spiritual Seeker goes silent, it's because he needs to process his sundry of thoughts; outside voices will only distract him from reaching truth inside his mind. If he can't reach conclusions for his thoughts, he can't process them; the 7 will linger on his thoughts endlessly until they confuse and frustrate him enough to want to act out. Faith equals redemption to the Spiritual Seeker. Believing in something—whether it's traditional Christianity or a pagan religion—can offer much-needed explanations to this primary number about the higher workings of the world.

Among nature is where the Spiritual Seeker feels most at ease. Here, he can recharge his intuitive batteries and enter an undisturbed state of serenity. The Spiritual Seeker is not one who yearns for human company; he feels content lying in a field of grass and simply listening to the rustle of leaves or deep-throated songs of birds. He takes great pleasure in observing and reflecting without always feeling the need to act. This life path thrives on simplicity and natural beauty, seeking what lightens the weight on his soul. For this reason, the 7 doesn't feel the need to be in a relationship simply for the sake of not being alone. To the Spiritual Seeker, being with the *right* partner is much more important than with *a* partner. At the same time, he acknowledges that having an equally passionate other half is vital to having a whole heart. He will fall in love with a partner who truly listens to his profound insight and helps him build a system of faith to make sense of this world and the next.

COMPATIBILITY FOR THE SPIRITUAL SEEKER

The Spiritual Seeker and the Independent (7 and 1)—likely to be in a stagnant relationship: Figuratively speaking, the partners in this relationship live on separate realms and view life from unrelated angles. The Independent is an animated, action-packed go-getter, while the Spiritual Seeker is a great philosopher of otherworldly matters. The Spiritual Seeker will analyze every aspect of the Independent's strengths and weaknesses, which will greatly annoy the Independent since his identity is tantamount to his existence. Simply put, the 1 does not want the 7 telling him what's wrong with him, especially from some mystical standpoint. When things turn sour, both partners can turn their backs on the other for a while: the Independent will think he's better off on his own, and the Spiritual Seeker will simply leave things up to fate. With this mentality, hell will freeze over before one reaches out to the other. This can result in lack of effort to maintain a serious relationship in time. These two individuals may have conflicting outlooks on life, but if each comes to appreciate and even learn from the other's way of thinking, they can create a beautiful balance between practicality and spirituality.

The Spiritual Seeker and the Introvert (7 and 2)—likely to be in a stagnant relationship: Both the Introvert and the Spiritual Seeker have a strong sense of intuition, which will attract them to one another; they will be drawn to each other's silent appeal. From there, it becomes the free will of both partners to make it work, because this relationship won't come without challenges: the Spiritual Seeker can be out of touch with the Introvert, who needs to feel strongly bonded to his partner at all times. The 7 is a step above the 2 in the field of metaphysics, always seeking the higher realities of life. The Introvert is more leveled with this world, enmeshed in his own thoughts and seeking comfort within himself by way of his emotions. If the Spiritual Seeker is not firm in his faith, the Introvert will feel as if his partner is being cynical, which can lead to their breakup. And if the Introvert refuses to open up to the Spiritual Seeker, the 7 won't spend too much time convincing him to do so. The Spiritual Seeker has to be aligned with the Introvert's feelings to keep his partner from feeling lonely in the relationship.

The Spiritual Seeker and the Extrovert (7 and 3)—likely to be in a transitory relationship: These partners can unveil new worlds to each other. The Spiritual Seeker is profound and probing in nature, and the Extrovert is superficial and upbeat. The Spiritual Seeker can inspire his partner to reach within and question his existence, while the Extrovert can teach his partner how to live in the present and enjoy the moment. A conversation between the 3 and 7 might consist of the Extrovert telling the Spiritual Seeker, "This is how it is," to which the Spiritual Seeker will respond, "But what if . . . ?" As long as each respects the other's opinions, theirs can be a long and lasting alliance. It will seriously offend his partner if one starts to think that his way of thinking and doing holds more merit than the other's; neither of these two archetypes likes to be critiqued or have their beliefs questioned. They will express different levels of communication that complement each other: the Extrovert can show the Spiritual Seeker how to release pent-up thoughts without restraint, and the Spiritual Seeker can guide the Extrovert to investigate his feelings without necessarily acting on them.

The Spiritual Seeker and the Realist (7 and 4)—likely to be in a stagnant relationship: This can be an interesting match, with each partner broadening the mindset of the other. The Realist is a rational, no-nonsense kind of person, while the Spiritual Seeker has fascinating ideas about this world and beyond. What results is a relationship in which, if each partner respects the other's viewpoints, new perspectives about the world can be gained: the 4 will realize that magic lies beyond the science of reasoning, and the 7 can acknowledge that practicality is sometimes the only way to advance in the real world. The Spiritual Seeker, however, will not hesitate to explore other options should he see that the Realist isn't requiting his efforts. The Realist wants to provide for his partner, but he needs to be given a nudge in the right direction and be told what would be most helpful. The Spiritual Seeker may not be able to provide this information since he's so often locked away in his own mind, and, truth be told, the Realist is equally closed off, planning but seldom doing. What's required of both partners is to search for solutions when discrepancies become too broad. The absence of excitement will be palpable in this relationship more than in many others.

The Spiritual Seeker and the Free Spirit (7 and 5)—likely to be in a stagnant relationship: The Free Spirit will be impressed by the Spiritual Seeker's unique take on the world and wealth of knowledge. The Spiritual Seeker will like that the Free Spirit can give him time alone. This couple gets great joy out of traveling together, the Spiritual Seeker to expand his knowledge of other cultures and belief systems and the Free Spirit for the sheer thrill of it. The problem, again, comes from the Free Spirit's inability to get attached for too long. The Spiritual Seeker will have to learn to tame the Free Spirit's wild side, or he'll be in for some unpleasant surprises: the 5 has a terrible tendency to vanish when things get tough. The Spiritual Seeker is just as free spirited as his partner, but he is able to commit to one person for the long run. The Free Spirit is more concerned with sensual pleasures, while the Spiritual Seeker wants to achieve serenity of the soul. In the true nature of a Spiritual Seeker, this archetype will try to analyze the Free Spirit in an attempt to figure him out. It is wise for these partners not to engage in verbal confrontation, since the 7 can be careless with his words and devastate the 5. This couple should work on their mutual interests and take every day as it comes, with each partner embracing the joys that his significant other can introduce into his life.

The Spiritual Seeker and the Hopeless Romantic (7 and 6)—likely to be in a transitory relationship: The Hopeless Romantic will be eager to sip from the Spiritual Seeker's fountain of knowledge, and the Spiritual Seeker will hold the cup steady for his thirsty partner. But the 6 will also have to learn to give the 7 the alone time he needs to do his research, deliberate, and regenerate his mind. Otherwise, the Spiritual Seeker might feel that the Hopeless Romantic is draining him of energy, and won't want to continue in a relationship in which he's being suffocated. This couple is passionate in the bedroom and should work on inventing new ways of pleasing each other. The Spiritual Seeker will selflessly encourage the Hopeless Romantic not to pay so much attention to him but to hone his own talents and skills; 7s wholeheartedly believe that each person should fulfill his purpose on Earth. If there is an archetype that can suppress the Hopeless Romantic's overgiving tendencies, it is the Spiritual Seeker, who will reassure his partner that he's entirely able to take care of himself, and has no problem coming second to the Hopeless Romantic's vocation.

The Spiritual Seeker and the Spiritual Seeker (7 and 7)—likely to be in a karmic relationship: Two Spiritual Seekers can set out on a quest that's out of this world (literally). They will feed each other unique ideas and profound perspectives. They just get each other's way of thinking, and that level of intimacy is invaluable. Spiritual Seekers tend to be loners unless they're paired with someone who comprehends them on a soulful level. There is a mutual sense of respect that's reserved for two partners with this life path: one respects the other's moods, philosophies, and opinions without question. They can remain silent for hours, each immersed in his own mind, without the need to interrupt the other's stream of thought. Two 7s are connected on a sentimental plane too; so much so, that if one is feeling off, the other may sense it from miles away. The drawback to this relationship is that if one does something to hurt the other, the wounds run just as deep as their bonds do. Spiritual Seekers heal slowly and remain affected by their partner's actions for a long time. It is vital for these partners to learn how to be practical as well as spiritual—they do live on planet Earth, after all.

The Spiritual Seeker and the Workaholic (7 and 8)—likely to be in a toxic relationship: One of the obvious issues in this relationship is that the Spiritual Seeker and the Workaholic vibrate at disparate levels: the 7 is concerned with his level of enlightenment, while the 8 is concerned with his level of income. One might never fully comprehend the other's way of being or understand why certain things are so crucial to him. The Spiritual Seeker won't get why his partner cares so much about material things, and the Workaholic won't regard spirituality as highly as his significant other. This can create a lack of emotional intimacy and drive a wedge between the partners, but not if each agrees to respect what's relevant to the other. If they can adopt a mentality of "to each his own," this couple becomes energetically complete: one will be the financial provider and the other will be the emotional provider. One can teach their children how to work hard in this world, and the other can show them how to access a greater awareness of our world—both are equally important to know. Each partner will have to verbally acknowledge his partner's hard work, whether that work brings money or the power of metaphysics.

The Spiritual Seeker and the Well-Rounded One (7 and 9)—likely to be in a complementary relationship: If the partners in this relationship are operating at their peak vibrations, this couple can fare quite well together. The Spiritual Seeker is profound, knowledgeable, and unconcerned with vanity, which the Well-Rounded One will admire. The Well-Rounded One is compassionate and on a mission to save the world, which the Spiritual Seeker will encourage. Focusing on their individual and shared aims will lead to much mental stimulation between these partners, keeping them engaged in positive activities and away from altercations. Problems creep in when either partner dips into lower energies: if the Spiritual Seeker acts like he knows it all or the Well-Rounded One gets caught up in family dramas, their dynamic can suffer. This will create petty, avoidable arguments that breed bigger dilemmas in time. If one partner takes a step back and gives his significant other some space, the 7 and 9 will soon return to normality and find a way to work things out. Both partners in this relationship know how to truly be there for one another, and that's enough to overcome whatever issues come up.

CHAPTER ELEVEN

LIFE PATH 8: THE WORKAHOLIC

Nothing depends on luck,
but all on good judgment
and diligence.

—Plutarch

WHETHER HE'S A HANDYMAN OR THE HEAD OF AMAZON, the Workaholic strives to achieve success. Fueled by the energy of 8, the Workaholic emphasizes the value of hard work and dedication. This life path has built his kingdom around his work, making his career into his life; it is an indivisible component of his identity in which he takes great pride. He chose his career long before he chose his significant other; when a partner does come into his life, she'll have to be supportive of his work. Even after he retires (which he'll do reluctantly), the Workaholic will continue partaking in his work in one way or another. The person who fits this archetype wants the best of both worlds, and he's not willing to compromise: he wants the successful job *and* the beautiful woman waiting for him at home. He is nearly—if not completely—addicted to his work because it delegates freedom and expression.

Under no circumstances can the Workaholic be with a stultifying, possessive partner who holds him back from his vocation. He sees the spouse who's constantly on top of him as a responsibility, not an asset, and he'll let go of a person who's not contributing to his growth, in the same way he'll fire an employee who's not performing up to his expectations. The Workaholic is captivated by a partner who labors to advance in her own career and keeps just as busy as he does. He gets along exquisitely well with a business-oriented individual who is also dutiful at home, though he often ends up with a homemaker. Although two Workaholics function well together, the female Workaholic doesn't have much time to cater to her husband, which can pose a problem since the male Workaholic needs all the assistance he can get from his companion.

The Workaholic is a no-nonsense kind of person who abides by a mind-over-matter mentality. Seeing is believing to the Workaholic, who considers words without actions little more than false promises. This is an admirably ambitious individual who believes in his powers and skills. He has an optimistic attitude and is confident he can achieve anything he wants. The Workaholic is in his natural element when he's at the head of a table moderating an important meeting, on set directing a movie scene by scene, or behind a podium delivering a rousing speech to an audience. Number 8 filters thoughts through the rational side of his mind, so his emotions often lose to logic. He can be pragmatic to the point of suppressing his sentiments or abandoning them altogether in favor of efficacy. This leads to a loss of playfulness and lightheartedness. The Workaholic takes his duties so seriously that he can treat his homelife like a job. In his mind he creates strict schedules even for his loved ones, allotting certain dates and times for playing with the kids, watching TV, even making love with his wife! He's so disciplined that play becomes disproportionate to work and leaves no room for spontaneity.

When he's away from his work for too long, the Workaholic starts to feel unproductive and exhibits symptoms of withdrawal, such as crashes in energy and hints of depression. In fact, the Workaholic may be putting in long hours to cover more than just the bills. Research shows there may exist a strong link between workaholism and ADHD, OCD, anxiety, and depression. Whether these psychiatric problems arise from extended work, or extended work is a means of coping with preexisting conditions, is unknown. The Workaholic doesn't always work because he finds it intrinsically pleasing, but because he feels an inner compulsion to work; his job may be his distraction from bothersome feelings or external pressures, or it may validate his worth to himself. In overworking himself, it's likely that the Workaholic is attempting to satisfy self-perceived shortcomings. As a child, the Workaholic may have been rigidly controlled and not granted enough liberty of thought. He might've grown up craving freedom of expression, settling on his work as a means of fulfillment and a way of dealing with things. Too much work signals not only emotional repression but can have dire repercussions on health. Burnout syndrome (BOS) is a work-related group of symptoms caused by heavy workload, long hours, diminished resources, and conflicts with coworkers, among other things. Chronic work-related stress will lead to energy depletion, a distant attitude toward one's work, and reduced personal accomplishment. When this happens, the Workaholic may ironically grow to despise his once-beloved work. Every Workaholic will experience occupational burnout sooner or later, and so can the average working person.

Not all 8s are CEOs of big companies; your own Workaholic might be a nurse, accountant, or car salesman who simply puts in too many hours and too much effort. As every Workaholic will have to learn, too much of a good thing is never a good thing. He needs to keep his work addiction in check, or he risks losing more-valuable aspects of life to it. The Workaholic can get his priorities mixed up, putting his ambitions before his children, his career before his health, and his money before his sanity. Life has a curious way of leading us back to the things that really matter, and sometimes this life path has to suffer a rather brutal wake-up call to regain sight of what's most important. One of the Workaholic's chief goals, therefore, should be to reassess what brings him joy, and to admit the fact that it might not be work related. This is a lesson not just for the Workaholic but for all of us. It is our right to be prosperous and abundant. We're allowed to have opulent and expensive things, but we shouldn't allow them to have us. Number 8 must enjoy what he works for in moderation, without letting it consume his heart or mind.

It's inevitable that his work will spill over onto his family. In psychology, displacement refers to an intense emotion that becomes internalized and then transferred onto a new object. The new object is usually unrelated to the cause of the emotion. If he had a bad day at work because a deal didn't go through, the Workaholic might come home and take his frustration out on his family members. He might become distant, cold, irritable, or aggressive. When this happens, the Workaholic needs to be reminded that his work is affecting his loved ones and that it must be separated from his homelife. Wait until the Workaholic isn't so caught up in the predicament, then propose this to him gently. If you bring it up when he's still brooding over the work issue, he might dismiss your argument and turn even moodier. Not all Workaholics have problems with their families due to their workloads.

Some are great at juggling a career, a family, and everything in between. If the Workaholic can find that sweet balance between commitment to his career and to his personal life, he and his partner can enjoy great synergy.

Most members of this archetype genuinely enjoy providing for those they love, and see to it that their family members are well cared for, accomplishing almost superhuman feats to give them all they need. The justification for his excessive work is his ability to bring good with it to those he loves. This doesn't, however, hold true for every person who embodies number 8. Because the Workaholic has learned (sometimes the hard way) the value of a hard-earned dollar, he might become parsimonious, even with his own partner. This is another aspect he must work on: maintaining a healthful, measured relationship with money so that he doesn't become possessed by avarice or megalomania. The Workaholic will regard the partner who can't accept his work as narrow minded or downright ungrateful if she's benefiting materially. He's turned on by a partner who's intelligent and focused like him. More than anything else, he appreciates the person who approves of his work and compels him to strive for even more.

The Workaholic can offer not only commitment but financial stability as well. The catch is that he must be doing well in his career. When this primary number is unstable in his work, his partner will feel the effects. He may work long hours or have a hectic schedule, but once he's attached to you, you will become a fundamental part of his life. Have patience with the Workaholic when his job requires time, but also know when to ask for his time. Because the 8 has a habit of getting carried away with long hours, there will be instances when you'll have to remind him to slow down and come home.

This life path's ideal relationship consists of teamwork and collaboration. He wants his partner to push him to finish a project and motivate him before a meeting. Assisting him in little ways will go a long way: create a schedule for his deadlines, pack his lunch on ultra-busy days, confirm his appointments, and so on. Ask about his day and offer advice when he needs it. Show the Workaholic that you admire his talents. He needs his other half to pay tribute to his work and, if possible, even help him at it. Though the Workaholic is more rational than romantic, he still needs an outlet to release emotions that become bottled up due to the demands of his career. Encourage him to talk, relax, and practice activities that discharge stress.

People interpret the Workaholic in one of two ways: they either accept his devotion to his work or they don't get it. The partner who can't come to terms with the Workaholic's full schedule will feel ignored and rejected, taking personally the time he spends away. The partner who grasps the importance of a Workaholic's career has a much-easier time coping with his frequent absences. We all like punctuality, but no one appreciates it more than number 8, whose time equals literal money. The Workaholic would like his significant other to handle her own problems and recognize how much he apprizes his career and how mindful he is of his professional duties. In turn, he'll share the rewards with his partner.

COMPATIBILITY FOR THE WORKAHOLIC

The Workaholic and the Independent (8 and 1)—likely to be in a transitory relationship: Discipline is the general vibration of this relationship. The Independent and Workaholic are well oriented in the real world and have their heads tightly fastened onto their shoulders. The diligence of each partner is impressive: the Independent is ever striving to improve himself, while the Workaholic is nearly obsessed with making material progress. They make an agreeable couple who respect each other's private needs and personal ambitions, but heaven forbid they start criticizing each other: harsh words can result in all-out war. The 8 sees himself as the boss of the relationship and, like an employer scolding his employee, will point out the 1's most painful failings. The Independent will not take lightly this direct sting to his identity. It may cause him to rethink the whole relationship and retreat into solitude once more. After that happens, each partner will start tending to his own goals, and their connection will diminish. They'll have to let each other win once in a while, with the Workaholic watching what he says so as not to bruise the Independent's ego. If these numbers want to last, they'll have to speak and act softly with each other.

The Workaholic and the Introvert (8 and 2)—likely to be in a transitory relationship: The Workaholic will take the lead in this relationship because he always needs a partner who follows him. The Introvert won't mind and will gladly allow his partner to go first, so long as the Workaholic recognizes his efforts. The Workaholic can at times be too straightforward with the Introvert and hurt his feelings without meaning to; this is the way of the 8, brutally honest because he believes in constructive criticism. He forgets that his partner is a delicate being and not a paid employee. When the 2 feels distraught, he will recede into his mind and become distant with his partner. If the Workaholic loses the trust he's worked hard to earn from the Introvert, it will prove nearly impossible to regain. To avoid this, the Workaholic must watch his words when addressing the Introvert, especially under tense emotions. He also needs to know when to pause work and applaud the Introvert's unique and detailed way of doing things. The energy between these partners should be kept in balance so that the Introvert doesn't feel beneath the Workaholic in any way.

The Workaholic and the Extrovert (8 and 3)—likely to be in a compromise relationship: An Extrovert and a Workaholic must find a greater reason to stay together, or they will quickly part ways. The 3 will feel neglected by the 8, who pores over his work and tasks night and day. Conversely, the Workaholic will feel frustrated by the Extrovert's lack of foundation and foggy vision for his future. Because his skill is communication, the Extrovert won't hold back when it comes to telling the Workaholic exactly how he feels and what his partner is doing wrong, which won't sit well with the Workaholic. He will retaliate by reminding the Extrovert of everything he's done for him and can even go as far as to deem him ungrateful. Because these life paths utter bitter words under strain, their conversations can turn sour and damage what could otherwise be a promising relationship. To ameliorate such situations, the Workaholic can gently press the Extrovert to dedicate himself to his projects, while the Extrovert can keep busy and let the Workaholic perform his work duties in peace. Both archetypes must learn to hold their tongues at times and express emotions in a less vitriolic way.

The Workaholic and the Realist (8 and 4)—likely to be in a karmic relationship: The Realist and Workaholic share core values that will help them remain together: loyalty, perseverance, and hard work are among the ideals these archetypes hold in high regard. They can build solid things owing to their principles, from a family to a business to a home. The Realist will lean on the Workaholic for little things, but the Workaholic will reject this tendency; he has a business to run and a career to attend to, and little time to resolve the minor inconveniences of his partner. The 8 appreciates when he's not bothered for every small matter, but the 4 wants to be aware of everything his partner is up to. One problem that might crop up is that the Workaholic doesn't have enough time to devote to the Realist, who is a needy archetype. When this happens, the Realist needs to address his concerns but also tend to his own goals. Stability is one of the key words that anchors these two life paths in reality and keeps them sane, and it is stability that can keep them thriving as a couple. When an earthquake strikes, such as a sudden loss or disaster, it can be hard for these numbers to regain firm ground. What the Realist and Workaholic must remember is to rely on each other to break through any adversity.

The Workaholic and the Free Spirit (8 and 5)—likely to be in a compromise relationship: Both these archetypes are energetic and animated, but not both can apply themselves thoroughly to their goals; only the Workaholic can do that. Under no circumstances will the 8 chase someone. The Workaholic will not put his work on pause to catch the runaway Free Spirit and tug him by the ear back to his relationship. He simply doesn't have time for that. Instead, he'll let the Free Spirit walk out the door if that's what he chooses to do. The Free Spirit, as we know, is not likely to settle down of his own accord unless his partner teaches him the merits of monogamy. The Free Spirit can be instrumental in aiding the Workaholic if he finds his partner's work interesting; he will gladly travel and meet with people on behalf of the Workaholic. Interestingly, both the 5 and 8 enjoy the finer things in life and splurge without glancing at the bill. One thing the Workaholic will appreciate is that the Free Spirit will give him the space he needs to tend to his career. The Free Spirit won't be on top of the Workaholic for every little thing, which would be a deal-breaker to the Workaholic. If the Free Spirit can settle down with a Workaholic without acting on that sudden whim to leave, these two life paths will call themselves a couple for a long time.

The Workaholic and the Hopeless Romantic (8 and 6)—likely to be in a complementary relationship: This relationship can work, especially in regard to the Hopeless Romantic aiding the Workaholic in his work duties. The Hopeless Romantic will feel important every time the Workaholic assigns him a task, and will set out to execute it at once. That said, the Workaholic also has to take care not to treat his partner like an assistant, and to remind himself that his other half is his equal, not the hired help. If the Hopeless Romantic is neglected by the Workaholic, he will feel hurt and push harder. This may irritate the Workaholic, who just wants to get his work done in peace and doesn't want to be asked, "What can I do for you?" several times a day. If the 8 mistreats the 6, the Hopeless Romantic will retreat into a world of doubt and self-blame, knowing it was "too good" to be true. A rebuffed 6 can even stray outside the relationship. If his partner's love and affection don't suffice, the Hopeless Romantic can turn his attention elsewhere and become infatuated with someone else. The Workaholic will think his partner is being ungrateful, especially if he provides financial aid to the Hopeless Romantic.

The Workaholic and the Spiritual Seeker (8 and 7)—likely to be in a toxic relationship: One of the obvious issues in this relationship is that the Spiritual Seeker and the Workaholic vibrate at disparate levels: the 7 is concerned with his level of enlightenment, while the 8 is concerned with his level of income. One might never fully comprehend the other's way of being or understand why certain things are so crucial to him. The Spiritual Seeker won't get why his partner cares so much about material things, and the Workaholic won't regard spirituality as highly as his significant other. This can create a lack of emotional intimacy and drive a wedge between the partners, but not if each agrees to respect what's relevant to the other. If they can adopt a mentality of "to each his own," this couple becomes energetically complete: one will be the financial provider and the other will be the emotional provider. One can teach their children how to work hard in this world, and the other can show them how to access a greater awareness of our world—both are equally important to know. Each partner will have to verbally acknowledge his partner's hard work, whether that work brings money or the power of metaphysics.

The Workaholic and the Workaholic (8 and 8)—likely to be in a karmic relationship: Two Workaholics fare well in business, so long as they're not greedy. If they choose to be in a relationship, they can be successful if they treat their partnership as a business: both Workaholics must perform their respective duties, like employees in a company. The problem is that no Workaholic wants to be a worker—he wants to be the boss. Each partner in this relationship will want to be in a higher position than the other, which can cause frequent conflicts and clashes of power. The key, as always, is compromise. The 8s will have to take turns giving in to each other. The Workaholic is excellent at performing his work, so if each partner is assigned specific tasks that don't interfere with the other's, the relationship is more likely to work. Two functioning Workaholics must conceive a sense of emotional intimacy together, since this archetype has trouble baring his soft and sensitive side even to those closest to him. Both 8s in this relationship will have to learn that being sweet, affectionate, and playful with your partner brings just as much satisfaction as being successful.

The Workaholic and the Well-Rounded One (8 and 9)—likely to be in a toxic relationship: The Workaholic and the Well-Rounded One live on two different levels of evolution: the Workaholic is concerned with his financial security, and the Well-Rounded one desires to undertake humanitarian efforts. If he's operating at a lower level of consciousness, the Workaholic can be selfish and avaricious, two traits the Well-Rounded One despises. In order for this relationship to work, the Workaholic will have to accept that he could stand to learn a thing or two from the Well-Rounded One; namely, that money doesn't bring true happiness (this is a hard pill for him to swallow, since he's dedicated his life to building a career that reaps significant material benefits). Where there's a will, there's a way, however, and no one knows this better than the Workaholic. If these two archetypes want to make it work, they can. It will take a bit of patience on the part of the Well-Rounded One, which he has plenty of, and a willingness from the Workaholic to be taught new lessons by his partner. If their minds work in tandem, they can achieve great things: the Workaholic can set up an organization that helps others, and the Well-Rounded One can fund or run that business.

CHAPTER TWELVE

LIFE PATH 9: THE WELL-ROUNDED ONE

What you leave behind is not what is engraved in stone monuments, but what is woven into the lives of others.

—Pericles

THE WELL-ROUNDED ONE WANTS TO LEAVE BEHIND A LEGACY, wishing to weave positivity into the lives of others. He is beyond ego or greed, and this is what sets him apart from most of the other life paths. Think of the Well-Rounded One as the least problematic and most reasonable kind of partner, and what the other archetypes aspire to become: healed, whole, and functional.

Number 9 is as dependable as it gets. He wants a legitimate relationship, and he's mentally and emotionally prepared for it. He can offer commitment without having to surmount the emotional and mental hurdles of the other primary numbers. The Well-Rounded One has completed his introspective work or he might not have obvious personality faults to begin with. His barriers are lifted; he is able to give and receive love without impediments. Any of the archetypes mentioned in this book can become loving, devoted partners if the right actions are taken, but the Well-Rounded One is already equipped. He has needs but isn't egoistic. He's not noticeably introverted or unusually independent. He knows when to step back from his work and refocus on his family. He neither holds on to unrealistic notions of love nor teeters on the edge of extremes.

The Well-Rounded One seeks solutions. He leaves no stone unturned in trying to resolve conflict. If you have an argument with a Well-Rounded One, expect that he'll want to settle it straightaway. Number 9 carefully tends to the emotional wellness he has cultivated, so although he will try to make the relationship work within reasonable means, once he has exhausted his efforts, he will let go of any partner who's proven to be toxic. He will try his best to find solutions for his relationship problems, but he won't forfeit his well-being for the sake of any person. Other archetypes can damage the Well-Rounded One: the Realist who asked for too much, the Workaholic who didn't pay enough attention, or the Free Spirit who didn't know what he wanted. Any well-rounded person can be broken down internally. Conversely, any archetype can become well rounded by performing the proper work.

Since the perfect person doesn't exist, the 9's partner will still have to adjust to a relationship with him. This life path can be vulnerable, hurt, reserved, selfish, or ambitious, but what makes him stand out is that he's not stuck being a certain way. His number one attribute is his malleability; being well rounded means being versatile, able to adapt to changes and challenges as they come. He's decent in all senses of the word and doesn't have layers of psychological complexities to comb through. The Well-Rounded One is not impulsive and doesn't jump to conclusions but takes time to work things out the right way. His fair and equitable nature means he can get along with most of the other archetypes.

The Well-Rounded One doesn't rely on the voices of outsiders, unless that voice is his partner's, whose opinion he esteems supremely. Unlike other archetypes who have trouble making the right decisions, the Well-Rounded One's conscience is über developed; his sense of right from wrong is nearly infallible. This is a morally upright life path who recognizes when he's transgressed and wants to right his wrongs. Others might try to take advantage of his righteousness and make the Well-Rounded One feel guilty to get their way (namely, his family members). This number is patient and tolerant, but don't mistake his kindness for weakness; he can be strong and fierce and certainly puts his foot down when necessary.

The Well-Rounded One enjoys being in control of things, but he must first be in control of himself. His ideal partner reinforces his mental and emotional equilibrium. To the 9, life is best when it's in balance. He values composure and order more than anyone. His mind is at ease when he has a mission and a sense of purpose. When the Well-Rounded One is under pressure or thrown off course, he becomes contemplative. He will retreat into himself to regain his steadiness, much like the Introvert and Spiritual Seeker tend to do. He craves a partner who not only compliments him but pushes him to become better each day. To win over the Well-Rounded One, you must show him that you are as equanimous as he is, and can contribute to his balance. The payoff is that in doing so, you will clear away old habits and emotions and become a better person too.

The Well-Rounded One prefers to walk away if he notices that you're self-absorbed, unrealistic, or covert and are unwilling to work on such tendencies. This number likes to commit to people he deems capable of commitment. He appreciates reliability because he's a person of his word, so you'll have to show him that you not only talk the talk but walk the walk. Self-control is the golden ticket to the Well-Rounded One's heart: be open with him without coming on too strongly, take the relationship seriously but don't rush into things, and be respectable without seeming uptight.

Unlike the Realist, who seizes the day for all its worth, the Well-Rounded One regards his life in the long term, weighing the possible pros and cons of each decision. Since he has a thorough understanding of the human matrix, if he sees that you have trouble keeping a job or friendships, he'll assume you'll have trouble keeping a relationship with him too. He protects himself, but not in an ego-induced way like the Realist; he simply wants a partner who can strengthen the mental, emotional, and physical stability he's worked hard to attain. The Well-Rounded One wants to know that you're *whole* on all levels: in your thoughts, emotions, and actions.

One of his defects is that the Well-Rounded One can take on too much, partly because everyone expects him to be able to handle it. This can make him feel overwhelmed, although he's unlikely to share his struggles with others. The 9 is human, after all, and as much as he may want to save the world, he needs to save himself first. His partner should encourage him to give his admirable but immense ambitions a rest until he recovers.

Sadly, the 9 also has a strange way of attracting family drama. He is too evolved to want to take part in any of it, but he somehow always gets caught up in the conflict: either feuding family members force him to take sides or they drag his name into the argument. The Well-Rounded One does not believe in fighting unless it's for the purpose of learning how to make up, so he suffers when there's dissent within his clan. Without intending to, he will carry the drama into the relationship with his partner. The Well-Rounded One must learn not to concede to turmoil, or he risks becoming a victim to it and wounded as a result. If he does become ensnared in family ordeals, the Well-Rounded One will be dragged down into the lower vibration of his life path and possibly become disassociated with time: he may start to live in the past, dwelling on the "could'ves" and "should'ves." The Well-Rounded One feels he could have done more because he is responsible to a fault, which evokes guilt and regret.

The Well-Rounded One strives to have a timeless and enduring relationship, the kind his parents might have had. As long as he can keep family problems at bay, this is a life path who embodies ethics and can sustain a truly healthful relationship; he teaches us that self-discipline, moderation, and integrity translate into positive relationships. If you're not a number 9, you must work to become more well rounded, regardless of your archetype—not for the person you love or to salvage your relationship, but for yourself.

COMPATIBILITY FOR THE WELL-ROUNDED ONE

The Well-Rounded One and the Independent (9 and 1)—likely to be in a soulmate relationship: This combination makes for an compelling couple that symbolizes two opposing sides of the personality spectrum. The Independent is ego driven, while the Well-Rounded One is propelled by altruism. The Independent dreams about advancing his own aspirations, while the Well-Rounded One dreams of contributing to the greater good. The Independent lives in the moment, while the Well-Rounded One thinks well into the future. Although their ambitions span in different directions, they have significant lessons to learn from each other: the Independent can learn how to focus on what really matters in life, while the Well-Rounded One can learn how to focus on what he wants to achieve for himself. Their common thread is that both partners seek solutions: they are motivated individuals determined to find a way forward, whether it's running a multimillion-dollar business or ending world hunger. Both the 1 and 9 thrive on solutions; they waste no time in resolving matters, and this applies to their relationship too. This, if nothing else, is enough to keep them together.

The Well-Rounded One and the Introvert (9 and 2)—likely to be in a complementary relationship: This is another match that can work beautifully. The Introvert can uplift the Well-Rounded One to become the greatest version of himself, and the Well-Rounded One can inspire the Introvert to hone his immense creative powers. These two partners can work well to embark on a meaningful project together, with the Introvert working out the finer details and the Well-Rounded One getting the message out to the world. Although the Well-Rounded One likes to put on a strong front, the Introvert will pick up on little things that might be bothering his partner, no matter how much the Well-Rounded One insists that he's fine; the 9 needs this sort of subtlety to remind him that people care about him as much as he cares about them. The Well-Rounded One wants to work for the greater good, but he might push himself beyond his limits in trying to do so. When this happens, the Introvert will reassure the Well-Rounded One that he's done more than enough, and prompt him to take a break. The 2 will treasure the 9's sense of integrity and honesty, which will empower the Introvert to reveal his innermost self without fear. This partnership is a good balance between working to improve yourself and working to improve the world.

The Well-Rounded One and the Extrovert (9 and 3)—likely to be in a complementary relationship: The beauty of this relationship is that the Well-Rounded One can teach the Extrovert how to expand his potential to do good and use his gift of gab for a greater purpose. In turn, the Extrovert will show the Well-Rounded One how to deliver his message to a larger audience and influence more people with his work. The Well-Rounded One's principle of altruism paired with the Extrovert's communicative creativity can mobilize this couple to start a campaign that's bigger than both of them; they can leave a legacy behind if their powers are used to enact positivity in the world. Both partners are social and demonstrative, and they do well when their conversations transcend gossip or trends. In the intimacy of their home, the 9 will push the 3 to analyze himself beneath his facade, while the 3 will defend the 9 through any family drama. Theirs will be a mostly peaceful relationship, but the Well-Rounded One is more likely to be loyal than the Extrovert. The Extrovert should aspire to reach the apex of self-control, as the Well-Rounded One has, for the sake of his own personal evolution.

The Well-Rounded One and the Realist (9 and 4)—likely to be in a compromise relationship: These two life paths make excellent planners, with the 4 thinking in the short term and the 9 thinking for the long term. The Realist can learn valuable lessons from his evolved partner about wisdom and compassion, virtues that span beyond logic and information. Perhaps the greatest one will come from following in his partner's footsteps and turning his dreams into actual decisions. In terms of needs, the Realist will expect the Well-Rounded One to wait on him, but the Well-Rounded One will be more concerned with the salvation of others. This is not to say the Well-Rounded One won't be sympathetic to the Realist; if there's one thing the Well-Rounded One has, it's empathy for those around him, in particular the partner he loves. Because the Well-Rounded One cares about the people in his life—as dysfunctional as they may be—the Realist must take care never to speak poorly of or insult his partner's family members. These are two intelligent archetypes, though one is more concerned with his own needs and the other with the needs of others. The 9 won't be impressed with the 4's conceitedness in the least. The Realist will have to be okay with the Well-Rounded One's concern for humanity and coming second for the sake of the greater good. If he is, then this couple can forge a way forward.

The Well-Rounded One and the Free Spirit (9 and 5)—likely to be in a complementary relationship: This is a relationship in which both partners allow each other to be themselves. The Well-Rounded One does not seek to alter the Free Spirit, as other archetypes do; instead, he invites the Free Spirit to express himself. The Free Spirit wishes to support the Well-Rounded One in his most noble endeavors, from starting a charity to opening a chain of shelters. This couple will love to travel, the Free Spirit to have new experiences and the Well-Rounded One to scope out areas where he can help those in need. But if the Well-Rounded One gets attached while the Free Spirit isn't completely convinced of his intentions, he risks being seriously hurt by the 5. The Well-Rounded One is loving but also realistic; he probably won't allow the Free Spirit a second chance, because he's wise enough to know that what his partner did once, he will do again. If the Well-Rounded One feels that the Free Spirit can't give him a serious relationship, he won't waste time trying to convince him otherwise. The best thing the 9 can do for the 5 is to help him settle down physically and emotionally so that their relationship has the greatest chances of success. In terms of chemistry, the Well-Rounded One will be instantly attracted to the Free Spirit's irresistible charm. The Free Spirit will savor the attention and get sucked in right away.

The Well-Rounded One and the Hopeless Romantic (9 and 6)—likely to be in a soulmate relationship: The sky's the limit for this match. The Hopeless Romantic will first be drawn to the Well-Rounded One's discipline and advanced sense of morality, and the Well-Rounded One to the Hopeless Romantic's pure and bold heart. The Hopeless Romantic's mind is rife with lofty ideas that he has trouble externalizing in the real world; they remain in the Hopeless Romantic's mind, and when he meets opposition to one, he swiftly moves on to the next. Thankfully, the Well-Rounded One can teach the Hopeless Romantic the patience and practicality that's needed to bring a dream to fruition. No life path can ground the Hopeless Romantic and persuade him to materialize his goals more than the Well-Rounded One, whose compassion and understanding are infinite. Under the auspices of the Well-Rounded One, the Hopeless Romantic's full potential can bloom. The 9's sense of fairness means he won't take advantage of his sacrificial 6 partner; he'll gently stop the Hopeless Romantic from overexerting himself in the relationship. In turn, the Hopeless Romantic will gift the Well-Rounded One with unconditional love and remain by his side under any circumstances. Only if they're living at low levels will they succumb to thinking the worst about each other.

The Well-Rounded One and the Spiritual Seeker (9 and 7)—likely to be in a complementary relationship: If the partners in this relationship are operating at their peak vibrations, this couple can fare quite well together. The Spiritual Seeker is profound, knowledgeable, and unconcerned with vanity, which the Well-Rounded One will admire. The Well-Rounded One is compassionate and on a mission to save the world, which the Spiritual Seeker will encourage. Focusing on their individual and shared aims will lead to much mental stimulation between these partners, keeping them engaged in positive activities and away from altercations. Problems creep in when either partner dips into lower energies: if the Spiritual Seeker acts like he knows it all or the Well-Rounded One gets caught up in family dramas, their dynamic can suffer. This will create petty, avoidable arguments that breed bigger dilemmas in time. If one partner takes a step back and gives his significant other some space, the 7 and 9 will soon return to normality and find a way to work things out. Both partners in this relationship know how to truly be there for one another, and that's enough to overcome whatever issues come up.

The Well-Rounded One and the Workaholic (9 and 8)—likely to be in a toxic relationship: The Workaholic and the Well-Rounded One live on two different levels of evolution: the Workaholic is concerned with his financial security, and the Well-Rounded one desires to undertake humanitarian efforts. If he's operating at a lower level of consciousness, the Workaholic can be selfish and avaricious, two traits the Well-Rounded One despises. In order for this relationship to work, the Workaholic will have to accept that he could stand to learn a thing or two from the Well-Rounded One; namely, that money doesn't bring true happiness (this is a hard pill for him to swallow, since he's dedicated his life to building a career that reaps significant material benefits). Where there's a will, there's a way, however, and no one knows this better than the Workaholic. If these two archetypes want to make it work, they can. It will take a bit of patience on the part of the Well-Rounded One, which he has plenty of, and a willingness from the Workaholic to be taught new lessons by his partner. If their minds work in tandem, they can achieve great things: the Workaholic can set up an organization that helps others, and the Well-Rounded One can fund or run that business.

The Well-Rounded One and the Well-Rounded One (9 and 9)—likely to be in a soulmate relationship: Two Well-Rounded partners make an excellent pair. Besides being highly functional, they will share an underlying drive to improve the world and should join forces in bringing about the positive changes they wish to see. Because they have expansive ideals and larger-than-life goals, it's essential for the Well-Rounded couple to take a step back and appreciate the little things together. They wish to change lives, but they mustn't get ahead of themselves; they should applaud themselves for the progress they've made instead of being harsh on themselves or one another. Number 9s are sensitive, old souls, so they will take to heart any criticism and minor insults. When they do have misunderstandings, Well-Rounded partners don't like to leave things unresolved. Whereas other partners might "sleep on it," this couple will take a brief time-out to ruminate, then return to settle the conversation almost immediately with prospective solutions. Since they've been gifted with a keen perception of human nature, Well-Rounded partners are not only sympathetic but also empathetic to each other. A word of caution: because 9s oftentimes experience rifts in their families, it is critical for this life path to keep external influences out of their relationship.

CHAPTER THIRTEEN

FREE WILL IN FATED RELATIONSHIPS

Happiness and freedom
begin with one principle.
Some things are within your
control and some are not.

—Heraclitus

THE CASE FOR FREE WILL IN COMPATIBILITY

As much as numbers affect our human relationships (sometimes more than we'd like), we mustn't underestimate the power of individual determination. I witnessed this truth in my own family. My mother was an Independent (1) and my father was a Spiritual Seeker (7). According to numerology and archetypes, this was not the most compatible match. But their free will reached further than formulas or personality types, and my parents decided to remain loyal to one another for 43 years, until their dying days. The model of a 1, my mother was hardheaded and practical. She was the commander of the household and delegated all matters within the family, not taking kindly to orders. My father, like a typical 7, was detached from the material world, curious about metaphysics, and sophic in thought. He would share wisdoms to rival even the Greeks! He often sat in his rocking chair and passed moments in peaceful contemplation while my mother berated him for some little thing he did wrong (personally, I think he tuned her out and didn't hear a word). My mother, who was as loving and caring as she could be for an unyielding 1, maintained a firm grip on her tough personality, while my father was unbothered and simply let her be who she was. My parents were the textbook definitions of their life paths, yet they shared a mutual love that was stronger than their archetypal differences.

This principle can work in reverse too. One of my clients, Alicia, was a Well-Rounded One (9), while her husband, Terrance, was a Hopeless Romantic (6). By the rules of numerology, they were a natural match and should have gotten along superbly. Even I was surprised when Alicia confessed that she and Terrance were having serious problems: constant arguments and outbreaks were driving an irreparable wedge into their relationship. It seems that Terrance, acting on free will fueled by his ego, was becoming distant and insensitive to Alicia. My client also discovered that not only was Terrance having an affair with another woman, but he had fathered a child with her. We found out that this woman was a 5, a toxic energy for Terrance. I told Alicia that her and her husband's bond wasn't destined to break, but that Terrance had made some very poor decisions.

The same may be said for you. Perhaps you're an impeccable match, but choosing to act on deception, pride, and obstinacy will cause your fated relationship to fall apart. Or you may be as incompatible as fire and ice, but if both of you have a burning desire to make it work, you certainly can. That's the magic dance between Earth and cosmos: our destiny was drafted by the divine, but we hold a pen in our hands. Despite the universal charm that numbers weave into our lives, we have the force of free will. Our volition can be miraculous if applied properly. Beyond our numbers and archetypes, we hold the liberty to make what we want of our relationships. This is an empowering truth. Before you reincarnated, you may have agreed to meet a certain person and get into a relationship with him, but if during your life you chose not to, or you chose to be with a different person instead, you're allowed to deviate from your destiny and amend this portion of your soul contract. You could be soulmates, but if neither of you performs your work, your relationship won't last too long. Or you could be unsuitable according to your numbers, but if you care about each other, you can negotiate through your differences with the right actions. Indeed, free will drastically impacts fated and nonfated relationships.

So what actions does it take to start a relationship as strongly as possible so that it has the best chances for success, beyond the influence of numbers? If you find yourself currently searching for a partner or in the incipient stages of romance, the first thing you should do is to understand what you need. You don't want to hurt anyone, including yourself, so you have to establish what it is that you need before entering a relationship: Do you need to have fun, have a family, or have something in between? If you don't really desire to be in a relationship, don't start one with a person who craves commitment. On the other hand, if you're looking for something serious, don't settle for a person whose dedication can span only a few nights. Know also that what you want and what you need can be two separate things: you might *want* to be single and party, but you might *need* a real relationship to nurture your personal growth and evolution. Through self-reflection, you can become aware of what's best for you.

The second key is to pick a person who's sincere, not just someone you're attracted to. A partner can come across as utterly sweet or charming in the beginning, but don't let first impressions fool you. Anyone can put on an "act," then quickly disappear once they've gotten into your pants or your bank account! The rule of thumb is to select a partner who is genuine rather than exciting (and if he's both, even better!). A person who has pure intentions won't pressure you into anything, physical or otherwise. Another positive indication is someone who is willing to help you when you need it most. An authentic partner will accept your flaws instead of trying to mold you to their liking.

It's equally important to choose to see beyond the season and not dismiss the potential of your relationship. It may have all the chances to flourish, but if you place restrictions on your budding romance, you'll make it temporary. Allow your relationship to thrive beyond the present and into the years ahead, letting it become what it's meant to become. A healthful human bond doesn't come with an expiration date, but it does come for a reason, whether to resolve karma or pass through certain experiences collectively. A good way to approach the role of your relationship is to answer two questions: *What has this person come into my life to teach me?* and *Can I realistically see a future with him?*

You'll also need to attract a partner who is available in all senses of the word. Being with a person who's already in a relationship, who's still fixed on a partner from his past, or who keeps his emotions locked up will cause you more complications than he's worth. Beware of becoming involved with a person who is emotionally unavailable, since this will leave you with the nagging feeling like something's missing. You deserve a partner who is there when you need him, just like you are for him.

Last but not least, you must perform your inner work. You could be dating for years, but if you're not truly ready for a relationship, your romance won't last. Before you can even think about beginning a relationship, you must perform your inner work: detach from the past, forgive others, clear your karma, and eradicate negative emotions. Once there's balance and harmony within you, you'll attract a relationship that reflects these qualities. Ask yourself, *Am I carrying any baggage from my past? Do I harbor resentment or anger toward an old partner? Have I received closure from former relationships?* Once you understand what's going on within you, the steps you have to take become evident.

THE THREE Cs OF ALL GOOD RELATIONSHIPS

Anyone whose relationship has lasted the test of time will tell you that successful human bonds require three Cs: compatibility, commitment, and compromise. These are values you'll have to apply to your relationship each day.

First, compatibility. In my practice I see many people entering a relationship for interest and not for the chemistry they share. A woman might marry a man for his money or status, and vice versa. But when two people aren't compatible and start a relationship for the wrong reasons, it is guaranteed to end in separation sooner or later.

Next comes commitment. As you may have learned from your own experiences, a relationship is no walk in the park! You become responsible for someone else's well-being, and you welcome that person into your most intimate zones. You must prepare to commit to your partner in the same way you commit to yourself—unconditionally.

Third is compromise. A relationship means letting someone else be right half of the time. Are you prepared for that? Not many people are ready to put their proud guard down, but compromise is the happy medium that keeps you together whether fate had it planned that way or not.

Without compatibility, commitment, and compromise, the bonds of a relationship are easily broken. Learning to look at your relationship through the lens of these three virtues will create a durable bond, in spite of your numbers and personality types.

BUILDING LOVE THAT THRIVES THROUGH TIME

Having a relationship is like having a house: you have to clean it, work on it, and improve it regularly. Maintaining a relationship entails that both partners are present each day—physically, emotionally, mentally, and spiritually. For love to last, it cannot remain stagnant; your relationship requires constant revision, like a poem that's never quite finished. The way you feel about each other will undoubtedly transform, both in good and bad ways, with time. This will require you to revisit your intentions and actions toward each other as they shift.

As you know, every couple's situation is unique, and some numbers get along better than others. But you can choose to adopt a supportive mentality to ensure the highest chances for success in your relationship. Here is some of my best guidance for crafting and keeping quintessential love:

Start from the beginning. Try to think back to the beginning of your relationship. Do you recall what made you fall in love with this person? What qualities made you interested in him, and no one else? These qualities are still alive in your partner, but they may be weighed down by negative emotions or bad habits. Look past his faults and dig deep to rediscover his greatest qualities, the ones you originally fell in love with.

Evaluate why you want to be in this relationship. Getting into a relationship and staying in a relationship are two different stepping-stones. Make a list of the ten reasons you want to stay in your relationship. They may range from comfort to love to habit, but they all are valid reasons because they matter to you. Revisit this list often, perhaps monthly or on special occasions such as your anniversary, and revise it as needed.

Make it us against the world. Make your bond unshakable by taking on an "us against the world" mentality. Holding on to the conviction that you and your significant other can rely on each other and will be there for one another unconditionally is the foundation for any relationship. No matter what life throws at you, know that you and your partner will get through it together. Affirm this each day, both to yourself and with your other half.

Keep work and home separate. My advice to my clients is to keep their personal life separate from their professional life. Many women have become career driven, which is an amazing feat. But problems from work can easily disrupt the energy of a relationship. Leave your stress at the office and disassociate your relationship from your job. This applies most to the Workaholic, but it can be a pertinent lesson to learn for any of the archetypes.

Forgive your partner when he's truly sorry. Your partner will make mistakes along the way; it's unavoidable. You must learn to forgive him (when he's genuinely sorry) and not automatically walk away. Some mistakes will be greater than others, but discerning giant errors from minor blunders is in your discretion. Will you be able to forgive your partner wholeheartedly? How will this affect your relationship in the future? Forgiving your partner also includes choosing to focus on the present and not reverting to what was or could have been. Remember, too, that if you pardon your partner's errors, he should do the same for you.

Recognize that people are not exchangeable. The independent and impulsive mentality of the modern world has taught us that people are interchangeable. We might say to ourselves, "This person has too many problems, so I'm going to change him for another one." Then, when the next partner shows his own fair share of problems, we realize this approach is flawed. Many people don't embrace their partner for his strengths and weaknesses alike; they embrace only what that person can do for them. We have to lose this belief if we want to keep up healthful relationships. No one is exchangeable, and when you realize this fact, you can work with your partner to find solutions instead of jumping into another relationship.

Keep your conscience clean. When in doubt, follow the Golden Rule: do unto others as you would have them do unto you. Keep your conscience clean by causing harm to no one and being of service whenever possible, including to your partner. This involves saying sorry when you're wrong and meaning your apology. Even if your partner does something wrong to you, you must continue to act in good faith for your own karma. Having a clean conscience lights up your path so that you can recognize when to stay in, change, or leave a relationship.

Balance your ego and higher self. One of the ways you can keep your conscience clean in your relationship is by balancing your ego and your higher self. The ego protects us, but it also creates discord between our emotions. That's because the ego disregards the "we" and emphasizes the "me." If left unchecked, it can easily push aside empathy to spotlight personal ambitions, which can spark emotions such as intolerance and selfishness. To keep your ego and higher self in harmony, I encourage you to practice self-care while also caring for others. This means tending to your own needs and desires while showing compassion for your partner.

Don't take everything so seriously. Most of us exaggerate our partner's idiosyncrasies in the greater scheme of things. Maybe your partner snores, forgets to put the toilet seat down, or can't cook to save his life. While annoying, these aren't reasons to ditch a relationship or leave an otherwise good person. Don't invent reasons for arguments that are negligible, or allow yourself to become irritated by every little quirk. Let your partner be who he is, and commend his advantages and deficiencies with equal acceptance. While you shouldn't take some things seriously, one thing you should take quite seriously is your other half: his needs, wishes, and struggles.

Envision your future. Don't take it day by day and hope that things will get better—be proactive! Don't be afraid to make changes in your relationship and stand up for yourself. Plan ahead, envisioning what your relationship will look like in 5, 10, even 20 years from now. What can you and your partner do today to make sure that you're still satisfied with each other many years ahead?

Make necessary changes. Many people let time pass by without acknowledging the ways in which they and their partner are changing. Then, down the road, they suddenly wake up and wonder why they're so dissatisfied. It's because they didn't pay enough attention to their relationship to make changes in the right time, and the problems piled up. Any relationship, no matter how stable, could be made better. Just as your car needs maintenance, so too does your relationship require tune-ups. Evaluate what needs to be addressed or corrected in some way, then consult with your partner. Maybe your partner doesn't trust you or gets jealous over little things. Make it a point to speak with him about this issue and find a way to rectify the matter from both sides.

Keep it simple. As human beings, we tend to complicate and convolute. As a rule of thumb, the simpler your relationship, the more authentic and long lasting it will be. Don't laden your relationship with false promises and pretentious demands, or you risk it falling apart. The rise of social media has led many couples to paint false portraits to the world, flaunting their lavish lifestyle to others but working very little on the progress of their relationship. You don't need to be the "hottest" couple in the neighborhood—this does nothing to increase your odds of having a successful relationship.

Worship with your partner. The family that prays together stays together. You should worship with each other even if you belong to different creeds. If your partner is Jewish and you're Christian, he can come to church with you and you can go to temple with him, so long as you're bolstering each other's beliefs systems. Solidifying your religious beliefs will deepen your relationship and bring you both closer to Spirit. Truly, there is something sublime about a faith-based connection.

Form healthful habits together. Take up a new habit with your partner, such as an exercise routine or a craft you know he'll love. This will spark conversation and tender moments that later become memories. Engaging in mutual interests jointly is an excellent way to grow closer and keep you away from negative tendencies. Studies reveal that what one partner does, the other will repeat. You're more likely to take up a healthful habit if your partner does it. This also applies to unhealthful habits, which is why it's essential to make sure you're undertaking behaviors that reduce stress, boost serenity, and offer a mutual sense of purpose.

Take time apart. Spending time apart from your partner is as important as spending time with him; it's healthful to take time for yourself not only to fulfill your needs but to make your partner miss you. The more often we see someone, the less the sensory part of our brain responds to his presence; we become "used" to them. Don't hesitate to take a week off from your relationship to visit relatives or take a trip with friends. You'll both feel more eager to be with each other after some time apart.

Prioritize your relationship. It's easy to let your relationship fall behind other responsibilities: work, school, kids, and other parts of a daily routine can put your love life on the back burner. While this is common, it's not a good indication. Your partner is the person with whom you decided to embark on a lifelong journey. He should, therefore, be one of the foremost elements of your life. Do you feel like you're ignoring your partner's needs or putting him on hold more and more often? If so, you'll have to revisit how you can juggle your obligations more efficiently to give your partner the attention he deserves (remember that he should be meeting your needs too!). In order to make a relationship work, you'll have to place it where it belongs, as one of your priorities.

Practice emotional intimacy. I always encourage my clients to practice emotional intimacy. This is perhaps the single most important piece of advice I give to others looking to enjoy a great relationship, no matter what number their significant other may be. Intimacy isn't restricted to intercourse. It reaches far deeper than physical and can be soulful. Emotional intimacy is the glue that keeps two people together: it's a deep mental exchange and intense bonding of the mind and spirit too. It is knowing what your partner needs before he even gets a chance to ask—feeling his emotions, needs, and desires as if they were your own. Emotional intimacy is much more powerful than physical intimacy because it delves deep into your loved one's fears and hopes. Being consistently *aware* of your partner is key. Maintain a sense of intimacy with him by paying attention to how he's behaving on a day-to-day basis. What's bothering him? What are his short- and long-term goals? Pay close attention to the person you like; ask him what he needs, how his day was, what his goals are, etc. Encourage him to communicate and open up to you. Set yourself up as a source of trust and support. This brings you closer and creates attachment. Recognize what it is that your partner needs most from you in that given moment—is it to be nurtured or left alone? If two people are not in sync emotionally, there is no moving forward. But when there exists emotional intimacy, the partners vibrate on the same frequency. Acknowledging your significant other's needs will keep you perfectly in tune as a couple.

Your numbers account for a good part of your compatibility, but your determination counts for even more. All relationships, effortless or exhausting, fated or forged from free will, can be fortified by taking actions that promote intimacy, empathy, and excitement.

APPENDIX:

QUICK REFERENCE GUIDES

Below you will find quick reference guides to life paths and archetypes, personal years, pinnacles, and the seven types of love relationships.

TABLE 1: LIFE PATHS AND ARCHETYPES

THE INDEPENDENT

Life path 1: independent, ambitious, and a born leader
Influence of number 1: attitude
Famous number 1s: Martin Luther King Jr., Larry King, Tom Hanks
Life path 1s are administrated by the sun, which rules our solar system. They hold the energy of leadership and acumen. Because of this energy, not only do 1s have lots of ideas, but they also have the self-discipline to carry them out. Ambitious and fearless, 1s are natural leaders. They like to learn and are often self-taught, then they like to pass on their knowledge to others. 1s are hardworking, smart, organized, neat, and extremely productive.

THE INTROVERT

Life path 2: emotional, reserved, and intuitive
Influence of number 2: introspection
Famous number 2s: Madonna, Barack Obama, Bill Clinton
Number 2s are represented by the moon, which reflects light from the sun and emits the maternal energy of cooperation, balance, partnership, and understanding. 2s tend to be good listeners and are diplomatic and tactful. They are often quiet, introverted, humble, intelligent, and calm. Those with a life path 2 work on realizing their dreams, heightening their intellect, keeping close relationships, and enjoying leisure time.

THE EXTROVERT

Life path 3: creative, outgoing, and charismatic
Influence of number 3: communication
Famous number 3s: Jennifer Lopez, Hillary Clinton, Barbara Walters
Number 3 carries the energy of Jupiter, the planet of courage, persuasion, hard work, energy, and knowledge. It is considered a lucky planet and bears a powerful energy. Life path 3 is the number of creativity, beauty, and "the good life." 3s are extroverted and gifted with eloquence and musical talents. They often have lovely voices and take up careers in the arts, media, or education. They are well informed, altruistic, and extravagant.

THE REALIST

Life path 4: orderly, pragmatic, and self-reliant
Influence of number 4: logic
Famous number 4s: Donald Trump, Bill Gates, Oprah Winfrey
Number 4 bears the energy of Uranus, the planet of discipline, grounding, and structure. 4s are active, dynamic, diplomatic, self-motivated, determined, caring, brave, and generous. They tend to have a good memory and a superior sense of dignity, which can make 4s seem a bit egoistic to outsiders. Those with a life path 4 know the merit of working hard to achieve wealth and power, and they often do so through inheritance or real estate.

THE FREE SPIRIT

Life path 5: free spirited, adventurous, and versatile
Influence of number 5: freedom
Famous number 5s: Abraham Lincoln, Angelina Jolie, Steven Spielberg

Number 5 is commanded by the planet Mercury, the energy of intellect, independence, and freedom. 5s are strong-willed risk takers who appreciate their freedom above all. They're intelligent beings with deep feelings, good physical energy, and strong intuition. 5s are understanding, progressive, and adaptable. Those within this life path are elevated thinkers who like to think—and step—outside the box; they have a penchant to travel, dabble in the arts, and attain luxurious objects.

THE HOPELESS ROMANTIC

Life path 6: empathetic, loving, and humble
Influence of number 6: sacrifice
Famous number 6s: Albert Einstein, Eleanor Roosevelt, George W. Bush
The energy of Venus leads number 6, the planet of service, responsibility, emotional harmony, and nurturing. 6s are kind, polite, soft spoken, funny, temperamental, friendly, humorous, sacrificial, and talkative. They have lots of ideas, an active mind, and a passion for life. 6s are concerned for others and possess a strong need to assist and serve. They simply adore the family life and feel an unfailing sense of duty toward members of their kin.

THE SPIRITUAL SEEKER

Life path 7: inquisitive, spiritual, and deep
Influence of number 7: knowledge
Famous number 7s: Princess Diana, Steven Hawking, Leonardo DiCaprio
The number 7 imbibes the energy of Neptune, the planet of wisdom, spirituality, intuition, and higher knowledge. 7s are logical and honest. They're immersive thinkers who love to unravel the mysteries of life and death. They are fun to be around, approachable, caring, forgiving, and sympathetic, and they love to be alone. They are aware of their profound nature and reject that which is without depth or meaning.

THE WORKAHOLIC

Life path 8: assertive, responsible, and determined
Influence of number 8: ambition
Famous number 8s: Pablo Picasso, Elizabeth Taylor, Penelope Cruz
Number 8 follows the energy of Saturn, the planet of karma. 8s are goal oriented, driven, motivated, and able to manifest success in the material world. They relish in having power and being in control, both over their circumstances and others. As leaders, they are good at supervising, managing, and making money. Those with a life path 8 are attractive, caring, suave, brave, firm, independent, and romantic.

THE WELL-ROUNDED ONE

Life path 9: balanced, humanitarian, and aware
Influence of number 9: empathy
Famous number 9s: Mahatma Gandhi, Whitney Houston, Elvis Presley
Number 9 is overseen by Mars and Pluto. This number exudes the energy of idealism, humanitarianism, altruism, unfaltering generosity, and sacrifice. 9s have a divine purpose and embrace their higher mission. Because they have the energy of Pluto, the planet of destruction, 9s endure much sorrow, illness, and loss, which lends them a greater understanding of life. For the most part, they're calm, clever, confident, and optimistic.

TABLE 2: PERSONAL YEARS

PERSONAL YEAR 1

This is a cardinal year because in personal year 1 you control your destiny more so than on any other occasion in your life. In this year, you are setting a course that will decide whether you will be happy or unhappy, successful or unsuccessful, in a relationship or single, over the next nine years. Whatever you plan this year will endure and have longevity. It is a time during which you will find it easier to summon your inner strength. Most importantly, this is the year to plant the seeds for the projects that are dearest to you, since they have the greatest chance of blossoming and bearing fruit. If you plant nothing now and wait until a year later, you will not yield the best possible crop. This is the most advantageous year to marry, begin a business, and start making major life changes, such as buying a home or making a significant geographical move.

PERSONAL YEAR 2

The second personal year is a time of delays and disappointments. In this year, the forces of the universe block your energy, thwarting even the most-well-constructed plans. The key to making it through this year is patience and acceptance. It is possible to lose something important during a year 2. It might be a friendship that goes sour or an opportunity that slips out of your hands. Despite these setbacks, personal year 2 is an excellent year for reconciliation in relationships. If you have been unable to make peace with someone, try to do so in this year. This is a period of germination and gestation, a slow-moving year that is favorable for planting seeds of love and new romance. Getting married in your personal year 2 is a good idea, although personal year 1 is the best time.

PERSONAL YEAR 3

This is a year of opportunities and pleasures. The accent is on beauty, harmony, and enjoyment. If you would like to end a relationship, this is the time to do so. If you marry during this time, you will be going against the energy of the year. Personal year 3 is generally a good year for generating income and saving money, but ill fitted for investments. For example, you might add a savings account to an account you already have, to deposit extra money, but this would not be a good time to invest that extra money in a business. It would be wiser to sell items you no longer need and accumulate material wealth rather than begin any financial ventures. This is also a great year for meeting people. Those you welcome into your life this year will encourage and enrich you. If possible, however, avoid entering into major commitments or intense friendships in this year. Projects started in personal year 3 are fated to be short lived. If you marry, open a business, or undertake a major task, such as quitting smoking or taking up a diet-and-exercise routine, you'll find yourself in a difficult struggle.

PERSONAL YEAR 4

Unlike the previous year, this is a year to nurture the plans you made in personal year 1 and watch your projects grow. It is an exceptional year to initiate a new relationship and work out old family problems. New friendships made in personal year 4 will be deep and long lasting, but endings to relationships will be problematic this year. If you divorce your spouse or leave your church or social group, the situation may turn rancorous. While beginnings involving family and relationships will work out well this year, other big changes will not. The universe will not back speculative investments or sudden job shifts. Because 4 and 8 are numbers of karma, personal year 4 is a year of facing the consequences of one's actions from the past. Personal year 4 is a time to step back and look at your life. Use this year to improve your home and your health, but without making major changes, such as buying a house or switching careers. Instead, work on self-discipline and overall organization.

PERSONAL YEAR 5

This is the year of change, a time that brings freedom from problems alongside opportunities to improve your life. Personal year 5 is a vacation period, a perfect time to travel and focus your mind on higher matters and ideals instead of being caught up in mundane, everyday trivialities. This is not the time to start a new business. Instead, year 5 has a vibration of fertility and pregnancy, and it's easiest to get pregnant in year 5. Your finances may fluctuate in this year, but overall they should remain steady. You can use the energy of this year to your advantage by keeping your mind open to new ways of doing things and expanding projects you already have underway. This year is also indicated for advertising, promotion, and fine-tuning what already exists in your life.

PERSONAL YEAR 6

This is the most pleasant of all years. It is a period of success. This is a year free of financial problems and a time to make adjustments to your work and come up with new ideas. You can also let go of projects that are not working for you during this time. Personal year 6 brings divine reinforcement. It has a domestic and positive vibration. This is a promising year for strengthening your relationship with your spouse and children and making improvements in your home. The energy of 6 supports your commitment to your family and sacred space. This is also a good year for healing wounds and making peace with your enemies. The vibration of personal year 6 is fortunate for the arts and for serving others. It is a time to thrive in all senses of the word.

PERSONAL YEAR 7

The Bible says that God created the world in six days and that on the seventh day, God rested. Similarly, personal year 7 is a time for you to rest and plan what you want to manifest in the upcoming personal year. This is a year of patience and waiting. Do not invest or plant the seeds for your future. Instead, meditate, travel, introspect, and examine the mistakes of the past so they don't repeat in future years. This is an occasion for solitude, peace, and wisdom. Do not force any issues or lose control; even if you do get your way, it will prove not to be in your favor. Avoid making any major moves this year and, if possible, stay in your home and at your current job.

PERSONAL YEAR 8

This is the year of karma, and the karmic impact can be felt twice as hard as in personal year 4 and when it comes to dealing with the fallout of past actions. Personal year 8 is a year of achievements and accomplishments, a time when you reap the material rewards of your efforts. Money will come from unexpected sources, and you will be presented with opportunities and recognition. It is an excellent time to look for a better job or embark on a new career altogether. This is a year for material prosperity, so ventures begun this year can work out well, especially if you begin them in the first six months of the year, when the energy of the year is strongest.

PERSONAL YEAR 9

Personal year 9 is a time to finish projects you have begun, and a time to resolve your karma if you did not do so in personal year 8. It is a year in which to let go of things and not to begin them. This is not a year to marry or produce a child. If you separate from your partner this year, reconciliation is highly unlikely. This is also the year to drop relationships and projects that have drained you during the past life cycle of nine years. It's a good time to study, write, and plan events for the next year. It is a period for getting your affairs in order and cleaning up after the harvest of personal year 8.

TABLE 3: PINNACLES

PINNACLE 1

The first pinnacle concerns soul searching and development. During this time, you explore questions about your personal existence, inner world, and spiritual growth. The first pinnacle ranges from birth to approximately age 30, depending on your soul code.

PINNACLE 2

The second pinnacle stretches from the age of 30 through 39. This is when you identify your larger purpose in life and begin to find your social responsibility. This pinnacle intensifies a need to become grounded, from finding a spouse and starting a family to forming a solid career.

PINNACLE 3

The third pinnacle lasts between ages 40 and 49. This is a time for increasing your personal power and gaining true financial stability. During this pinnacle, you typically work on advancing your career and succeeding materially, as well as securing a legacy for future generations.

PINNACLE 4

The fourth pinnacle debuts at age 50 and spans throughout the next 30 years. During this time, you learn to maintain balance between work and leisure, between caring for others and caring for yourself. Work starts to take a back seat to self-care during this pinnacle, and life slows down.

TABLE 4: SEVEN TYPES OF LOVE RELATIONSHIPS

TRANSITORY

Most likely to happen in personal years 3, 5, and 9
Most likely to develop between life paths 3 and 7, and 1 and 8

A transitory relationship acts as a bridge between two phases of evolution, enacting change or easing transitions. Transitory relationships are marked by desire, physical chemistry, excitement, and adventure, but they lack commitment and authentic love. The partners in this kind of relationship generally don't become too attached and can let go of each other without much trouble. No serious sacrifices or advancements are made in a transitory relationship.

TOXIC

Most likely to happen in personal years 5, 7, and 9
Most likely to develop between life paths 5 and 6, and 7 and 8

A toxic relationship is the most problematic of the seven and the one with the lowest vibrational energy. It is like trying to mix water and oil; you can stir them as much as you'd like, but the two substances will never blend. Toxic relationships occur when two primary numbers who are simply not meant to be together try to defy all odds. Moreover, by being careless, negligent, and inconsistent, any two people can turn a relationship toxic.

STAGNANT

Most likely to happen in personal years 3, 5, and 8
Most likely to develop between life paths 5 and 7, and 2 and 9

A stagnant relationship can start off great and steadily expand until it reaches a plateau it can't get past. This is the defining feature of this type of relationship: hitting a brick wall that makes everything stop in its tracks. It's not necessarily that the partners did anything wrong or that they're not performing the right work, but that the relationship has reached its spiritual capacity and cannot advance any further.

COMPROMISE

Most likely to happen in personal years 2, 7, and 9
Most likely to develop between life paths 2 and 9, and 7 and 9

A compromise relationship is the most common of the seven types. It occurs when two people form a union based on an arrangement of comfort, such as financial stability or social standing. Many relationships that are meant to end continue because both partners have become so used to each other that they find it difficult to part ways; they settle for one other. Relationships based on compromise keep us stuck in a comfort zone.

COMPLEMENTARY

Most likely to happen in personal years 2, 3, and 6
Most likely to develop between life paths 2 and 4, and 3 and 6

Complementary relationships are harmonious and uplifting in nature, with each partner balancing the other physically, emotionally, and mentally. They can still compromise in the sense of coming together for mutual interests such as finances, but there is a special spark in this type of relationship that's not present in a compromise. Relationships that are complementary are usually for the long term or lifelong.

KARMIC

Most likely to happen in personal years 1, 4, and 8
Most likely to develop between life paths 4 and 8, and 8 and 8

A karmic bond involves some sort of action that must unfold within the relationship, such as the breaking of behavioral patterns or cycles of events. This type of relationship denotes past lives shared by two partners; hence a strong feeling of familiarity or "knowing." Two souls that have passed through certain experiences together will find each other again to close what was left open. A karmic relationship is almost always described as intense.

SOULMATE

Can happen in any personal year, but most likely to happen in personal years 1 and 6
Most likely to develop between life paths 1 and 9, and 9 and 9

A soulmate relationship is a one-of-a-kind bond reaching deeper than physical or emotional levels. Soulmate relationships are far and few, but when they do occur, they often last the test of time. This kind of relationship is marked by a profound connection between two people, one that may even be difficult to convey. Soulmates just get each other: they can finish each other's sentences, are best friends as well as lovers, and share an "us against the world" mentality.

ACKNOWLEDGMENTS

I would like to thank Amy Zerner and Monte Farber for their kindness and generosity, as well as my three guardian angels: Sanda, Victor, and Virgil.

ALSO BY CARMEN HARRA, PHD

Committed: Finding Love and Loyalty through the Seven Archetypes (with Alexandra Harra). Red Bank, NJ: Newman Springs, 2021.

The Karma Queens' Guide to Relationships: The Truth about Karma and Relationships (with Alexandra Harra). New York: TarcherPerigree / Penguin Books, 2015.

Wholeliness: Embracing the Sacred Unity That Heals Our World. Carlsbad, CA: Hay House, 2011.

The Eleven Eternal Principles: Accessing the Divine Within. Berkeley, CA: Crossing Press, 2009.

The Trinity of Health: Align Body, Mind and Soul in Order to Achieve Health and Happiness for Your Whole Life. BookSurge, 2007.

Decoding Your Destiny. Hillsboro, OR: Beyond Words, 2006.

Everyday Karma: A Renowned Psychic Shows You How to Change Your Life by Changing Your Karma. New York: Ballantine Books / Random House, 2002.